AFTER FINITUDE

Also available from Continuum:

Being and Event, Alain Badiou (translated by Oliver Feltham)
Infinite Thought, Alain Badiou (edited and translated by Oliver Feltham and Justin Clemens)
Theoretical Writings, Alain Badiou (edited and translated by Ray Brassier and Alberto Toscano)

AFTER FINITUDE

An Essay on the Necessity of Contingency

Quentin Meillassoux

Translated by Ray Brassier

continuum

Continuum

Continuum International Publishing Group
The Tower Building
11 York Road
London SE1 7NX

80 Maiden Lane
Suite 704
New York
NY 10038

www.continuumbooks.com

Liberté • Égalité • Fraternité
RÉPUBLIQUE FRANÇAISE

This book is supported by the French Ministry of Foreign Affairs as part of the Burgess programme run by the Cultural Department of the French Embassy in London. (www.frenchbooknews.com)

Originally published in French as *Après la finitude* @ Editions du Seuil, 2006

The English language translation © Continuum 2008

First published 2008
Reprinted 2009
Paperback edition 2009

British Library Cataloguing-in-Publication Data
A catalogue record for this book is available from the British Library.

ISBN: PB: 978–1–4411–7383–6

Library of Congress Cataloging-in-Publication Data

A catalog record for this book is available from the Library of Congress.

Typeset by Fakenham Photosetting Limited, Fakenham, Norfolk
Printed and bound in Great Britain by MPG Books Ltd, Bodmin, Cornwall

Contents

Preface

I

The purpose of the series 'The Philosophical Order'[1] is not only to publish mature and accomplished works of contemporary philosophy, or indispensable philosophical documents from every era, but also essays in which it is possible to detect the sense of something new – texts which respond to the question: 'What wound was I seeking to heal, what thorn was I seeking to draw from the flesh of existence when I became what is called "a philosopher"?' It may be that, as Bergson maintained, a philosopher only ever develops one idea. In any case, there is no doubt that the philosopher is born of a single question, the question which arises at the intersection of thought and life at a given moment in the philosopher's youth; the question which one must at all costs find a way to answer. This is the category to which we must assign this book by Quentin Meillassoux.

II

This brief essay, which is a fragment from a particularly important philosophical (or 'speculative', to use the author's own vocabulary) enterprise, returns to the root of the problem which provided the impetus for Kant's critical philosophy; the problem which, through the solution which Kant proposed, can be said to have broken the history of thought in two. This problem, which Hume formulated most clearly, pertains to the necessity of the laws of nature. From whence does this putative necessity arise, given that perceptual experience, which is the source of everything we know or think we know about the world, provides no guarantee whatsoever for it?

Kant's response, as we know, grants to Hume that everything we know comes from experience. Yet Kant upholds the necessity of the laws of nature, whose mathematical form and conformity to empirical observation we have known since Newton, concluding that since this necessity cannot have arisen from our sensible receptivity, it must have another source: that of the constituting activity of a universal subject, which Kant calls 'the transcendental subject'. This distinction between empirical receptivity and transcendental constitution appears to be the obligatory framework for all modern thought, and in particular for every attempt to think the nature of 'modalities', such as necessity or contingency. The latter continue to be the objects of Deleuze's or Foucault's reflections. But they also underlie the distinction, which is fundamental for Carnap and the analytic tradition, between formal and empirical sciences.

Quentin Meillassoux demonstrates with astonishing force how another interpretation of Hume's problem – one which has remained occluded, even though it is more 'natural' – leads to a completely different resolution. Like Kant, Meillassoux saves necessity, including logical necessity. But like Hume, he grants that there is no acceptable ground for the necessity of the laws of nature.

Meillassoux's proof – for it is indeed a proof – demonstrates that there is only one thing that is absolutely necessary: that the laws of nature are contingent. This entirely novel connection between contrary modalities puts thought in a wholly other relation to the experience of the world; a relation which simultaneously undoes the 'necessitarian' pretensions of classical metaphysics as well as the 'critical' distribution of the empirical and the transcendental.

Quentin Meillassoux then goes on to draw some of the consequences of his resumption of the fundamental problem ('what can I know?') towards two other problems: 'what must I do?' and 'what can I hope?' It is there that what lies beyond finitude is deployed for contemporary thinkers.

It would be no exaggeration to say that Quentin Meillassoux has opened up a new path in the history of philosophy, hitherto conceived as the history of what it is to know; a path that circumvents Kant's canonical distinction between 'dogmatism', 'scepticism' and 'critique'. Yes, there is absolute logical necessity. Yes, there is radical contingency. Yes, we can think what there is, and this thinking in no way depends upon a supposedly constituting subject.

This remarkable 'critique of Critique' is presented here without embellishment, cutting straight to the heart of the matter in a particularly lucid and argumentative style. It allows thought to be destined towards the absolute once more, rather than towards those partial fragments and relations in which we complacently luxuriate while the 'return of the religious' provides us with a fictitious supplement of spirituality.

Alain Badiou

Chapter 1
Ancestrality

The theory of primary and secondary qualities seems to belong to an irremediably obsolete philosophical past. It is time it was rehabilitated. For the contemporary reader, such a distinction might appear to be a piece of scholastic sophistry, devoid of any fundamental philosophical import. Yet as we shall see, what is at stake in it is the nature of thought's relation to the absolute.

First of all, what does it consist in? The terms 'primary quality' and 'secondary quality' come from Locke, but the basis for the distinction can already be found in Descartes.[1] When I burn myself on a candle, I spontaneously take the sensation of burning to be in my finger, not in the candle. I do not touch a pain that would be present in the flame like one of its properties: the brazier does not burn itself when it burns. But what we say of affections must likewise be said of sensations: the flavour of food is not savoured by the food itself and hence does not exist in the latter prior to its ingestion. Similarly, the melodious beauty of a sonic sequence is not heard by the melody, the luminous colour of a painting is not seen by the coloured pigment of the canvas, and so on. In short, nothing sensible – whether it be an affective or perceptual quality – can exist in the way it is given to me in the thing by itself, when it is not related to me or to any other living creature. When one thinks about this thing 'in itself', i.e. independently of its relation to me, it seems that none of these qualities can subsist. Remove the observer, and the world becomes devoid of these sonorous, visual, olfactory, etc., qualities, just as the flame becomes devoid of pain once the finger is removed.

Yet one cannot maintain that the sensible is injected by me into things like some sort of perpetual and arbitrary hallucination. For there is indeed a constant link between real things and their sensations: if there were no *thing* capable of giving rise to the sensation of redness, there would be no perception of a red thing; if there were no real fire, there would be no sensation of burning. But it makes no sense to say that the redness or the heat can exist as qualities just as well without me as with me: without the *perception* of redness, there is no red thing; without the sensation of heat, there is no heat. Whether it be affective or perceptual, the sensible only exists as a *relation*: a relation between the world and the living creature I am. In actuality, the sensible is neither simply 'in me' in the manner of a dream, nor simply 'in the thing' in the manner of an intrinsic property: it is the very relation between the thing and I. These sensible qualities, which are not in the things themselves but in my subjective relation to the latter – these qualities correspond to what were traditionally called *secondary qualities*.

Yet it is not these secondary qualities that discredited the traditional theory of qualities. That it makes no sense to attribute to the 'thing in itself' (which is basically the 'thing without me') those properties which can only come about as a result of the relation between the thing and its subjective apprehension has effectively become a commonplace which few philosophers have contested. What has been vigorously contested, in the wake of phenomenology, is the way in which Descartes or Locke conceived of such a relation: as a modification of thinking substance tied to the mechanical workings of a material body, rather than, for instance, as a noetico-noematic correlation. But it is not a question of taking up once more the traditional conception of the constitutive relation of sensibility: all that matters for us here is that the sensible *is* a relation, rather than a property inherent in the thing. From this point of view, it is not particularly difficult for a contemporary philosopher to agree with Descartes or Locke.

This ceases to be the case as soon as one brings into play the core of the traditional theory of properties, viz., that there are *two types* of property. For what decisively discredited the distinction between primary and secondary qualities is the very idea of such a distinction: i.e. the assumption that the 'subjectivation' of sensible properties (the emphasis on their essential link to the presence of a subject) could be restricted to the object's sensible determinations, rather than extended to *all* its conceivable properties. By 'primary qualities', one understands properties which are supposed to be inseparable from the object, properties which one supposes to belong to the thing even when I no longer apprehend it. They are properties of the thing as it is without me, as much as it is with me – properties of the in-itself. In what do they consist? For Descartes, they are all of those properties which pertain to extension and which are therefore subject to geometrical proof: length, width, movement, depth, figure, size.[2] For our part, we will avoid invoking the notion of extension, since the latter is indissociable from sensible representation: one cannot imagine an extension which would not be coloured, and hence which would not be associated with a secondary quality. In order to reactivate the Cartesian thesis in contemporary terms, and in order to state it in the same terms in which we intend to uphold it, we shall therefore maintain the following: *all those aspects of the object that can be formulated in mathematical terms can be meaningfully conceived as properties of the object in itself.* All those aspects of the object that can give rise to a mathematical thought (to a formula or to digitalization) rather than to a perception or sensation can be meaningfully turned into properties of the thing not only as it is with me, but also as it is without me.

The thesis we are defending is therefore twofold: on the one hand, we acknowledge that the sensible only exists as a subject's relation to the world; but on the other hand, we maintain that the mathematizable properties of the object are exempt from the constraint of such a relation, and that they are effectively in the object in the way in which I conceive them, whether I am in relation with this object or not. But before we proceed to justify this thesis, it is necessary to understand in what regard it may seem absurd to a contemporary philosopher – and to root out the precise source of this apparent absurdity.

The reason why this thesis is almost certain to appear insupportable to a contemporary philosopher is because it is resolutely *pre-critical* – it seems to represent a regression to the 'naïve' stance of dogmatic metaphysics. For what we have just claimed is that thought is capable of discriminating between those properties of the world which are a function of our relation to it, and those properties of the world as it is 'in itself', subsisting indifferently of our relation to it. But we all know that such a thesis has become indefensible, and this not only since Kant, but even since Berkeley.[3] It is an indefensible thesis because thought cannot get *outside itself* in order to compare the world as it is 'in itself' to the world as it is 'for us', and thereby distinguish what is a function of our relation to the world from what belongs to the world alone. Such an enterprise is effectively self-contradictory, for at the very moment when we think of a property as belonging to the world in itself, it is precisely the latter that we are thinking, and consequently this property is revealed to be essentially tied to our thinking about the world. We cannot represent the 'in itself' without it becoming 'for us', or as Hegel amusingly put it, we cannot 'creep up on' the object 'from behind' so as to find out what it is in itself[4] – which means that we cannot know anything that would be beyond our relation to the world. Consequently, the mathematical properties of the object cannot be exempted from the subjectivation that is the precondition for secondary properties: they too must be conceived as dependent upon the subject's relation to the given – as a form of representation for the orthodox Kantian, or as an act of subjectivity for the phenomenologist, or as a specific formal language for the analytical philosopher, and so on. But in every case, any philosopher who acknowledges the legitimacy of the transcendental revolution – any philosopher who sees himself as 'post-critical' rather than as a dogmatist – will maintain that it is naïve to think we are able to think *something* – even if it be a mathematical determination of the object – while abstracting from the fact that it is invariably we who are thinking that something.

Let us note – for we will have occasion to return to this point – that the transcendental revolution consisted not only in disqualifying the naïve realism of dogmatic metaphysics (for Berkeley's subjective idealism had already accomplished this), but also and above all in redefining objectivity outside of the dogmatic context. In the Kantian framework, a statement's conformity to the object can no longer be defined in terms of a representation's 'adequation' or 'resemblance' to an object supposedly subsisting 'in itself', since this 'in itself' is inaccessible. The difference between an objective representation (such as 'the sun heats the stone') and a 'merely subjective' representation (such as 'the room seems warm to me') is therefore a function of the difference between two types of subjective representation: those that can be universalized, and are thus by right capable of being experienced by everyone, and hence 'scientific', and those that cannot be universalized, and hence cannot belong to scientific discourse. From this point on, *intersubjectivity*, the consensus of a community, supplants the *adequation* between the representations of a solitary subject and the thing itself as the veritable criterion of objectivity, and of scientific objectivity more particularly. Scientific truth is no longer what conforms to an in-itself supposedly indifferent to the way in which it is given to the subject, but rather what is susceptible of being given as shared by a scientific community.

Such considerations reveal the extent to which the central notion of modern philosophy since Kant seems to be that of *correlation*. By 'correlation' we mean the idea according to which we only ever have access to the correlation between thinking and being, and never to either term considered apart from the other. We will henceforth call *correlationism* any current of thought which maintains the unsurpassable character of the correlation so defined. Consequently, it becomes possible to say that every philosophy which disavows naïve realism has become a variant of correlationism.

Let us examine more closely the meaning of such a philosopheme: 'correlation, correlationism'.

Correlationism consists in disqualifying the claim that it is possible to consider the realms of subjectivity and objectivity independently of one another. Not only does it become necessary to insist that we never grasp an object 'in itself', in isolation from its relation to the subject, but it also becomes necessary to maintain that we can never grasp a subject that would not always-already be related to an object. If one calls 'the correlationist circle' the argument according to which one cannot think the in-itself without entering into a vicious circle, thereby immediately contradicting oneself, one could call 'the correlationist two-step' this other type of reasoning to which philosophers have become so well accustomed – the kind of reasoning which one encounters so frequently in contemporary works and which insists that

it would be naïve to think of the subject and the object as two separately subsisting entities whose relation is only subsequently added to them. On the contrary, the relation is in some sense primary: the world is only world insofar as it appears to me as world, and the self is only self insofar as it is face to face with the world, that for whom the world discloses itself [...][5]

Generally speaking, the modern philosopher's 'two-step' consists in this belief in the primacy of the relation over the related terms; a belief in the constitutive power of reciprocal relation. The 'co-' (of co-givenness, of co-relation, of the co-originary, of co-presence, etc.) is the grammatical particle that dominates modern philosophy, its veritable 'chemical formula'. Thus, one could say that up until Kant, one of the principal problems of philosophy was to think substance, while ever since Kant, it has consisted in trying to think the correlation. Prior to the advent of transcendentalism, one of the questions that divided rival philosophers most decisively was 'Who grasps the true nature of substance? He who thinks the Idea, the individual, the atom, God? Which God?' But ever since Kant, to discover what divides rival philosophers is no longer to ask who has grasped the true nature of substantiality, but rather to ask who has grasped the more originary correlation: is it the thinker of the subject-object correlation, the noetico-noematic correlation, or the language-referent correlation? The question is no longer 'which is the proper substrate?' but 'which is the proper correlate?'

During the twentieth century, the two principal 'media' of the correlation were consciousness and language, the former bearing phenomenology, the latter the various currents of analytic philosophy. Francis Wolff has very accurately described consciousness and language as 'object-worlds'.[6] They are in fact unique objects insofar as they 'make the world'. And if these objects make the world, this is because from their perspective 'everything is inside' but at the same time 'everything is outside ...' Wolff continues:

> Everything is inside because in order to think anything whatsoever, it is necessary to 'be able to be conscious of it', it is necessary to say it, and so we are locked up in language or in consciousness without being able to get out. In this sense, they have no outside. But in another sense, they are entirely turned towards the outside; they are the world's window: for to be conscious is always to be conscious of something, to speak is necessarily to speak about something. To be conscious of the tree is to be conscious of the tree itself, and not the idea of the tree; to speak about the tree is not just to utter a word but to speak about the thing. Consequently, consciousness and language enclose the world within themselves only insofar as, conversely, they are entirely contained by it. We are in consciousness or language as in a transparent cage. Everything is outside, yet it is impossible to get out.[7]

What is remarkable about this description of the modern philosophical conception of consciousness and language is the way in which it exhibits the paradoxical nature of correlational exteriority: on the one hand, correlationism readily insists upon the fact that consciousness, like language, enjoys an originary connection to a radical exteriority (exemplified by phenomenological consciousness transcending or as Sartre puts it 'exploding' towards the world); yet on the other hand this insistence seems to dissimulate a strange feeling of imprisonment or enclosure within this very exteriority (the 'transparent cage'). For we are well and truly imprisoned within this outside proper to language and consciousness given that we are *always-already* in it (the 'always already' accompanying the 'co-' of correlationism as its other essential locution), and given that we have no access to any vantage point from whence we could observe these 'object-worlds', which are the unsurpassable providers of all exteriority, from the outside. But if this outside seems to us to be a cloistered outside, an outside in which one may legitimately feel incarcerated, this is because in actuality such an outside is entirely relative, since it is – and this is precisely the point – relative to us. Consciousness and its language certainly transcend themselves towards the world, but there is a world only insofar as a consciousness transcends itself towards it. Consequently, this space of exteriority is merely the space of what faces us, of what exists only as a correlate of our own existence. This is why, in actuality, we do not transcend ourselves very much by plunging into such a world, for all we are doing is exploring the two faces of what remains a face to face – like a coin which only knows its own obverse. And if contemporary philosophers insist so adamantly that thought is entirely oriented towards the outside, this could be because of their failure to come to terms with a bereavement – the denial of a loss concomitant with the abandonment of dogmatism. For it could be that contemporary philosophers have lost the *great outdoors*, the *absolute* outside of pre-critical thinkers: that outside which was not relative to us, and which was given as indifferent to its own givenness to be what it is, existing in itself regardless of whether we are thinking of it or not; that outside which thought could explore with the legitimate feeling of being on foreign territory – of being entirely elsewhere.

Finally, in order to round off this brief exposition of the post-critical philosopheme, we must emphasize that the correlation between thought and being is not reducible to the correlation between subject and object. In other words, the fact that correlation dominates contemporary philosophy in no way implies the dominance of philosophies of *representation*. It is possible to criticize the latter in the name of a more originary correlation between thought and being. And in fact, the critiques of representation have not signalled a break with correlation, i.e. a simple return to dogmatism.

On this point, let us confine ourselves to giving one example: that of Heidegger. On the one hand, for Heidegger, it is certainly a case of pinpointing the occlusion of being or presence inherent in every metaphysical conception of representation and the privileging of the present at-hand entity considered as object. Yet on the other hand, to think such an occlusion at the heart of the unconcealment of the entity requires, for Heidegger, that one take into account the *co-propriation* (*Zusammengehörigkeit*) of man and being, which he calls *Ereignis*.[8] Thus, the notion of *Ereignis*, which is central in the later Heidegger, remains faithful to the correlationist exigency inherited from Kant and continued in Husserlian phenomenology, for the 'co-propriation' which constitutes *Ereignis* means that neither being nor man can be posited as subsisting 'in-themselves', and subsequently entering into relation – on the contrary, both terms of the appropriation are originarily constituted through their reciprocal relation: 'The appropriation appropriates man and Being to their essential togetherness.'[9] And the ensuing passage clearly exhibits Heidegger's strict observance of the correlationist 'two-step':

We always say *too little* of 'being itself' when, in saying 'being', we omit its essential presencing *in the direction* of the human *essence* and thereby fail to see that this essence itself is part of 'being'. We also say *too little* of the human being when, in saying 'being' (not being human) we posit the human being as independent and then first bring what we have thus posited into a relation to 'being'.[10]

At this stage, we can begin to take stock of the number of decisions that it behoves every philosopher to uphold – whatever the extent of her break with modernity – should she not wish to regress to a merely dogmatic position: the correlationist circle and two-step; the replacement of adequation by intersubjectivity in the redefinition of scientific objectivity; the maintaining of the correlation even in the critique of representation; the cloistered outside. These postulates characterize every 'post-critical' philosophy, i.e. every philosophy that sees itself as sufficiently faithful to Kantianism not to want to return to pre-critical metaphysics.

It is with all these decisions that we are breaking when we maintain the existence of primary qualities. Are we then bent on deliberately regressing to dogmatism? Moreover, what is it that incites us to break with the circle of correlation?

***

It's just a line. It can have different shades, a little like a spectrum of colours separated by short vertical dashes. Above these are numbers indicating immense quantities. It's a line the like of which one finds in any work of scientific popularization. The numbers designate dates and these dates are principally the following:

- the date of the origin of the universe (13.5 billion years ago)
- the date of the accretion of the earth (4.56 billion years ago)
- the date of origin of life on earth (3.5 billion years ago)
- the date of the origin of humankind (*Homo habilis*, 2 million years ago)

Empirical science is today capable of producing statements about events anterior to the advent of life as well as consciousness. These statements consist in the dating of 'objects' that are sometimes older than any form of life on earth. These dating procedures were called 'relative' so long as they pertained to the positions of fossils relative to one another (they were arrived at mainly by studying the relative depths of the geological strata from which the fossils were excavated). Dating became 'absolute' with the perfection of techniques (basically in the 1930s) that allowed scientists to determine the actual duration of the measured objects. These techniques generally rely upon the constant rate of disintegration of radioactive nuclei, as well as upon the laws of thermoluminescence – the latter permitting the application of dating techniques to the light emitted by stars.[11]

Thus contemporary science is in a position to precisely determine – albeit in the form of revisable hypotheses – the dates of the formation of the fossils of creatures living prior to the emergence of the first hominids, the date of the accretion of the earth, the date of the formation of stars, and even the 'age' of the universe itself.

The question that interests us here is then the following: *what is it* exactly that astrophysicists, geologists, or paleontologists are talking about when they discuss the age of the universe, the date of the accretion of the earth, the date of the appearance of pre-human species, or the date of the emergence of humanity itself? How are we to grasp the *meaning* of scientific statements bearing explicitly upon a manifestation of the world that is posited as anterior to the emergence of thought and even of life – *posited, that is, as anterior to every form of human relation to the world?* Or, to put it more precisely: how are we to think the meaning of a discourse which construes the relation to the world – that of thinking and/or living – as a fact inscribed in a temporality within which this relation is just one event among others, inscribed in an order of succession in which it is merely a stage, rather than an origin? How is science able to think such statements, and in what sense can we eventually ascribe truth to them?

Let us define our terms:

- I will call 'ancestral' any reality anterior to the emergence of the human species – or even anterior to every recognized form of life on earth.
- I will call 'arche-fossil' or 'fossil-matter' not just materials indicating the traces of past life, according to the familiar sense of the term 'fossil', but materials indicating the existence of an ancestral reality or event; one that is anterior to terrestrial life. An *arche*-fossil thus designates the material support on the basis of which the experiments that yield estimates of ancestral phenomena proceed – for example, an isotope whose rate of radioactive decay we know, or the luminous emission of a star that informs us as to the date of its formation.

Let us proceed then from this simple observation: today's science formulates a certain number of ancestral statements bearing upon the age of the universe, the formation of stars, or the accretion of the earth. Obviously it is not part of our remit to appraise the reliability of the techniques employed in order to formulate such statements. What we are interested in, however, is understanding under what conditions these statements are meaningful. More precisely, we ask: *how is correlationism liable to interpret these ancestral statements?*

We need to introduce a distinction at this point. There are in fact two basic types of correlationist thought, just as there are two basic types of idealism. For the correlation can be posited as unsurpassable either from a transcendental (and/or phenomenological) perspective, or a speculative one. It is possible to maintain the thesis according to which all that we can ever apprehend are correlates, or the thesis according to which the correlation as such is eternal. In the latter case, which is that of the *hypostasis* of the correlation, we are no longer dealing with correlationism in the strict sense of the term, but with a metaphysics that eternalizes the Self or the Mind, turning the latter into the perennial mirror for the manifestation of the entity. From the latter perspective, the ancestral statement presents no particular difficulty: the metaphysician who upholds the eternal-correlate can point to the existence of an 'ancestral witness', an attentive God, who turns every event into a phenomenon, something that is 'given-to', whether this event be the accretion of the earth or even the origin of the universe. But correlationism is not a metaphysics: it does not hypostatize the correlation; rather, it invokes the correlation to curb every hypostatization, every substantialization of an object of knowledge which would turn the latter into a being existing in and of itself. To say that we cannot extricate ourselves from the horizon of correlation is not to say that the correlation could exist by itself, independently of its incarnation in individuals. We do not know of any correlation that would be given elsewhere than in human beings, and we cannot get out of our own skins to discover whether it might be possible for such a disincarnation of the correlation to be true. Consequently, the hypothesis of the ancestral witness is illegitimate from the viewpoint of a strict correlationism. Thus the question we raised can be reformulated as follows: once one has situated oneself in the midst of the correlation, while refusing its hypostatization, how is one to interpret an ancestral statement?

Let us remark first of all that the meaning of ancestral statements presents no problem for a dogmatic philosophy such as Cartesianism. Consider what an ancestral event would mean for a physicist familiar with the *Meditations*. She would begin with the following observation: in the case of an event occurring prior to the emergence of life on earth, such as the accretion of the earth (i.e. the era of the accumulation of matter which gave rise to the formation of our planet), it makes no sense to say that 'it was hot then', or that the light was 'blinding', or to make any other subjective judgements of this type. Since we do not know of any observer who was there to experience the accretion of the earth – and since we do not even see how a living observer would have been able to survive had she experienced such heat – all that can be formulated about such an event is what the 'measurements', that is to say, the mathematical data, allow us to determine: for instance, that it began roughly 4.56 billion years ago, that it did not occur in a single instant but took place over millions of years – more precisely, tens of millions of years – that it occupied a certain volume in space, a volume which varied through time, etc. Accordingly, it would be necessary to insist that it makes no sense to claim that those qualities that occur whenever a living creature is present – such as colour (rather than wavelength), heat (rather than temperature), smell (rather than chemical reactions), etc. – that those *secondary* qualities were present at the moment of the accretion of the earth. For these qualities represent the modes of relation between a living creature and its environment and cannot be relevant when it comes to describing an event that is not only anterior to every recognized form of life but incompatible with the existence of living creatures. Consequently, our Cartesian physicist will maintain that those statements about the accretion of the earth which can be mathematically formulated designate actual properties of the event in question (such as its date, its duration, its extension), even when there was no observer present to experience it directly. In doing so, our physicist is defending a Cartesian thesis about matter, but not, it is important to note, a Pythagorean one: the claim is not that the being of accretion is inherently mathematical – that the numbers or equations deployed in the ancestral statements exist in themselves. For it would then be necessary to say that accretion is a reality every bit as ideal as that of number or of an equation. Generally speaking, statements are ideal insofar as their reality is one of signification. But their referents, for their part, are not necessarily ideal (the cat is on the mat is real, even though the statement 'the cat is on the mat' is ideal). In this particular instance, it would be necessary to specify: the *referents* of the statements about dates, volumes, etc., existed 4.56 billion years ago as described by these statements – but not these statements themselves, which are contemporaneous with us.

But let us be more precise. A scientist would not state categorically that an ancestral event definitely occurred in the way in which she has described it – that would be imprudent. For we know – at least since Popper – that every theory advanced by empirical science is by right revisable: it can be falsified and supplanted by one that is more elegant, or that exhibits greater empirical accuracy. But this will not prevent the scientist from considering that it makes sense to *suppose* that her statement is true: that things could actually have happened the way she has described them and that so long as her description has not been supplanted by another theory, it is legitimate to assume the existence of the event such as she has reconstructed it. And in any case, even if her theory is falsified, this can only be by another theory which will also be about ancestral events, and which will also be supposed to be true. Thus, from a Cartesian perspective, ancestral statements are statements whose referents can be posited as real (albeit in the past) once they are taken to have been validated by empirical science at a given stage of its development.

All this allows us to say that, on the whole, Cartesianism accounts rather satisfactorily for the scientist's own conception of her discipline. We could even wager, without taking too much of a risk, that where the theory of qualities is concerned, scientists are much more likely to side with Cartesianism than with Kantianism: they would have little difficulty in conceding that secondary qualities only exist as aspects of the living creature's relation to its world – but they would be much less willing to concede that (mathematizable) primary qualities only exist so long as we ourselves exist, rather than as properties of things themselves. And the truth is that their unwillingness to do so becomes all too understandable once one begins to seriously examine how the correlationist proposes to account for ancestrality.

For let us be perfectly clear: from the perspective of the correlationist, the interpretation of ancestral statements outlined above is inadmissible – or at least, inadmissible so long as it is interpreted *literally*. Doubtless, where science is concerned, philosophers have become modest – and even prudent. Thus, a philosopher will generally begin with an assurance to the effect that her theories in no way interfere with the work of the scientist, and that the manner in which the latter understands her own research is perfectly legitimate. But she will immediately add (or say to herself): legitimate, *as far as it goes*. What she means is that although it is normal, and even natural, for the scientist to adopt a spontaneously realist attitude, which she shares with the 'ordinary person', the philosopher possesses a specific type of knowledge which imposes a correction upon science's ancestral statements – a correction which seems to be minimal, but which suffices to introduce us to another dimension of thought in its relation to being.

Consider the following ancestral statement: 'Event Y occurred x number of years before the emergence of humans.' The correlationist philosopher will in no way intervene in the content of this statement: she will not contest the claim that it is in fact event Y that occurred, nor will she contest the dating of this event. No – she will simply add – perhaps only to himself, but add it he will – something like a simple codicil, always the same one, which he will discretely append to the end of the phrase: event Y occurred x number of years before the emergence of humans – *for humans* (or even, for *the human scientist*). This codicil is the codicil of modernity: the codicil through which the modern philosopher refrains (or at least thinks she does) from intervening in the content of science, while preserving a regime of meaning external to and more originary than that of science. Accordingly, when confronted with an ancestral statement, correlationism postulates that there are at least *two levels of meaning* in such a statement: the immediate, or realist meaning; and the more originary correlationist meaning, activated by the codicil.

What then would be a literal interpretation of the ancestral statement? The belief that the realist meaning of the ancestral statement *is its ultimate meaning* – that there is *no* other regime of meaning capable of deepening our understanding of it, and that consequently the philosopher's codicil is irrelevant when it comes to analysing the signification of the statement. Yet this is precisely what the correlationist cannot accept. For suppose for a moment that the realist or Cartesian interpretation harboured the key to the ultimate meaning of the ancestral statement. We would then be obliged to maintain what can only appear to the post-critical philosopher as a tissue of absurdities; to wit (and the list is not exhaustive):

- that *being* is not co-extensive with *manifestation*, since events have occurred in the past which were not manifest to anyone;
- that what *is* preceded *in time* the *manifestation* of what is;
- that manifestation itself emerged in time and space, and that consequently manifestation is not the *givenness of a world*, but rather an intra-worldly occurrence;
- that this event can, moreover, be dated;
- that thought is in a position *to think manifestation's emergence in being*, as well as a being or a time anterior to manifestation;
- that the fossil-matter is the givenness *in the present* of a being that is *anterior to givenness*; that is to say, that an arche-fossil manifests an entity's anteriority *vis-à-vis* manifestation.

But for the correlationist, such claims evaporate as soon as one points out the self-contradiction – which she takes to be flagrant – inherent in this definition of the arche-fossil: *givenness of a being anterior to givenness*. 'Givenness of a being' – here is the crux: being *is not* anterior to givenness, it *gives itself* as anterior to givenness. This suffices to demonstrate that it is absurd to envisage an existence that is anterior – hence chronological, into the bargain – to givenness itself. For givenness is primary and time itself is only meaningful insofar as it is always-already presupposed in humanity's relation to the world. Consequently, for the correlationist, there are indeed two levels at which ancestrality can be approached, each corresponding to the double occurrence of the term 'givenness' in the statement above, to wit: being gives itself (occurrence 1) as anterior to givenness (occurrence 2). At the first, superficial level, I forget the originary nature of givenness, losing myself in the object and naturalizing givenness by turning it into a property of the physical world, one that is liable to appear and disappear in the same way as a thing (being gives itself *as anterior to givenness*). But at the deeper level (being *gives itself* as anterior to givenness), I grasp that the correlation between thought and being enjoys logical priority over every empirical statement about the world and intra-worldly entities. Thus I have no difficulty reconciling the thesis of the *chronological* anteriority of what is over what appears – this being the level of meaning that is superficial, realist, derivative – with the thesis of the *logical* priority which givenness enjoys *vis-à-vis* what is given in the realm of givenness (to which the aforementioned chronological anteriority belongs) – the latter thesis corresponding to the deeper, more originary level, which alone is truly correct. I then cease to believe that the accretion of the earth straightforwardly preceded in time the emergence of humanity, the better to grasp that the status of the statement in question is more complex. This statement, properly understood, can be formulated as follows: 'The present community of scientists has objective reasons to consider that the accretion of the earth preceded the emergence of hominids by x number of years.'

Let us analyse this formulation.

We said above that, since Kant, objectivity is no longer defined with reference to the object in itself (in terms of the statement's adequation or resemblance to what it designates), but rather with reference to the possible universality of an objective statement. It is the intersubjectivity of the ancestral statement – the fact that it should by right be verifiable by any member of the scientific community – that guarantees its objectivity, and hence its 'truth'. It cannot be anything else, since its referent, taken literally, is *unthinkable*. If one refuses to hypostatize the correlation, it is necessary to insist that the physical universe could not *really* have preceded the existence of humans, or at least of living creatures. A world is meaningful only as given-to-a-living (or thinking)-being. Yet to speak of 'the emergence of life' is to evoke the emergence of manifestation amidst a world that pre-existed it. Once we have disqualified this type of statement, we must confine ourselves strictly to what is given to us: not the unthinkable emergence of manifestation within being, but the universalizable given of the present fossil-material: its rate of radioactive decay, the nature of stellar emission, etc. According to the correlationist, an ancestral statement is true insofar as it is founded upon an experiment that is in the *present* – carried out upon a given fossil-material – and also *universalizable* (and hence by right verifiable by anyone). It is then possible to maintain that the statement is true, insofar as it has its basis in an experience which is by right reproducible by anyone (universality of the statement), without believing naïvely that its truth derives from its adequation to the effective reality of its referent (a world without a givenness of the world).

To put it in other words: for the correlationist, in order to grasp the profound meaning of the fossil datum, one should not proceed from the ancestral past, but from the correlational present. This means that we have to carry out *a retrojection of the past on the basis of the present*. What is given to us, in effect, is not something that is anterior to givenness, but merely something that is given in the present but gives itself *as* anterior to givenness. The logical (constitutive, originary) anteriority of givenness over the being of the given therefore enjoins us to subordinate the apparent sense of the ancestral statement to *a more profound counter-sense*, which is alone capable of delivering its meaning: it is not ancestrality which precedes givenness, but that which is given in the present which retrojects a *seemingly* ancestral past. To understand the fossil, it is necessary to proceed from the present to the past, following a logical order, rather than from the past to the present, following a chronological order.

Accordingly, any attempt to refute dogmatism forces two decisions upon the philosopher faced with ancestrality: the doubling of meaning, and retrojection. The deeper sense of ancestrality resides in the logical retrojection imposed upon its superficially chronological sense. Try as we might, we do not see any other way to make sense of the arche-fossil while remaining faithful to the injunctions of the correlation.

Now, why is this interpretation of ancestrality obviously insupportable? Well, to understand why, all we have to do is ask the correlationist the following question: *what is it that happened 4.56 billion years ago? Did the accretion of the earth happen, yes or no?*

In one sense, yes, the correlationist will reply, because the scientific statements pointing to such an event are objective, in other words, inter-subjectively verifiable. But in another sense, no, she will go on, because the referent of such statements cannot have existed in the way in which it is naïvely described, i.e. as non-correlated with a consciousness. But then we end up with a rather extraordinary claim: *the ancestral statement is a true statement*, in that it is objective, but *one whose referent cannot possibly have actually existed in the way this truth describes it*. It is a true statement, but what it describes as real is an impossible event; it is an 'objective' statement, but it has no conceivable object. Or to put it more simply: *it is a non-sense*. Another way of saying the same thing is to remark that if ancestral statements derived their value solely from the current universality of their verification they would be completely devoid of interest for the scientists who take the trouble to validate them. One does not validate a measure just to demonstrate that this measure is valid for all scientists; one validates it in order to determine what is measured. It is because certain radioactive isotopes are capable of informing us about a past event that we try to extract from them a measure of their age: turn this age into something unthinkable and the objectivity of the measure becomes devoid of sense and interest, indicating nothing beyond itself. Science does not experiment with a view to validating the universality of its experiments; it carries out repeatable experiments with a view to external referents which endow these experiments with meaning.

Thus the retrojection which the correlationist is obliged to impose upon the ancestral statement amounts to a *veritable* counter-sense with respect to the latter: *an ancestral statement only has sense if its literal sense is also its ultimate sense*. If one divides the sense of the statement, if one invents for it a deeper sense conforming to the correlation but contrary to its realist sense, then far from deepening its sense, one has simply cancelled it. This is what we shall express in terms of the ancestral statement's *irremediable* realism: either this statement has a realist sense, and *only* a realist sense, or it has no sense at all. This is why a consistent correlationist should stop 'compromising' with science and stop believing that she can reconcile the two levels of meaning without undermining the content of the scientific statement which she claims to be dealing with. There is no possible compromise between the correlation and the arche-fossil: once one has acknowledged one, one has thereby disqualified the other. In other words, the consistent correlationist should stop being modest and dare to assert openly that she is in a position to provide the scientist with an *a priori* demonstration that the latter's ancestral statements are *illusory*: for the correlationist knows that what they describe can never have taken place the way it is described.

But then it is as if the distinction between transcendental idealism – the idealism that is (so to speak) urbane, civilized, and reasonable – and speculative or even subjective idealism – the idealism that is wild, uncouth, and rather extravagant – it is as if this distinction which we had been taught to draw – and which separates Kant from Berkeley – became blurred and dissolved in light of the fossil-matter. Confronted with the arche-fossil, *every variety of idealism converges and becomes equally extraordinary* – every variety of correlationism is exposed as an extreme idealism, one that is incapable of admitting that what science tells us about these occurrences of matter independent of humanity effectively occurred as described by science. And our correlationist then finds herself dangerously close to contemporary creationists: those quaint believers who assert today, in accordance with a 'literal' reading of the Bible, that the earth is no more than 6,000 years old, and who, when confronted with the much older dates arrived at by science, reply unperturbed that God also created at the same time as the earth 6,000 years ago those radioactive compounds that seem to indicate that the earth is much older than it is – in order to test the physicists' faith. Similarly, might not the meaning of the arche-fossil be to test the philosopher's faith in correlation, even when confronted with data which seem to point to an abyssal divide between what exists and what appears?

***

We will now consider two correlationist rejoinders to the ancestral objection, in order to render the latter more precise and to underline its singularity.

1) The first rejoinder proceeds by trivializing the problem of the arche-fossil, identifying it with a familiar and inconsequential anti-idealist argument. Our opponent will formulate it as follows:

'Your objection can easily be reduced to a hackneyed argument. First I note that your thesis arbitrarily privileges temporal seniority, whereas spatial distance would raise exactly the same difficulty (or rather the same semblance of difficulty) for correlationism. An event occurring in an immensely distant galaxy, beyond the reach of every possible observation, would in effect provide the spatial analogue for the event occurring prior to terrestrial life. In both cases, what we are dealing with are events devoid of possible witnesses (or at least of terrestrial ones), which is precisely the core of your argument, since the latter claims that correlationism cannot think that which cannot be connected to a relation-to-the-world. We should therefore be entitled to extend to space an argument which has hitherto been restricted to time, and adjoin the question of the distant to the question of the ancient.

'But then – and this is the second stage in our argument – we would notice that the notions of 'distance' or 'ancientness' are both vague, since no one can settle once and for all, in the context of this argument, where "the proximate" or "the recent" end, and where the "the distant" or "the ancestral" begin. Above all, we would immediately notice that the question of the relative proximity of the object under consideration becomes irrelevant to the force of the argument once the scope of the latter has been extended to space. Thus, for example, craters observed on the moon are actually 'closer' to us, from the viewpoint of the argument under consideration, than a vase falling in a country house when there is nobody there. The observed craters, in effect, pose no problem whatsoever to correlationism, since they are connected to a subject who apprehends them, whereas according to you the fallen vase would pose such a problem, since it went un-witnessed. Similarly, by your lights, a recent but un-witnessed temporal event is more problematic than an ancient event which has been registered in the commemorative experience of some consciousness or other.

'Consequently, your argument boils down to a particular variant of a trivial objection against idealism. One starts from the premise that what is un-witnessed is un-thinkable, unless it be by realism. And given that the ancestral event is by definition un-witnessed, since it is anterior to all terrestrial life, one easily concludes that it is un-thinkable for correlationism. But not only is this refutation of correlationism unoriginal, it is also grossly inadequate. For the *lacunary* nature of the given has never been a problem for correlationism. One only has to think of Husserl's famous 'givenness-by-adumbrations' [*Abschattung*]: a cube is never perceived according to all its faces at once; it always retains something non-given at the heart of its givenness. Generally speaking, even the most elementary theory of perception will insist on the fact that the sensible apprehension of an object always occurs against the backdrop of the un-apprehended, whether it be with regard to the object's spatiality or its temporality. Thus the visual perception of the sea presupposes the non-perception of its depths; the waves which we hear in the morning are heard against the backdrop of our not-hearing of the waves from the night before, etc.

'Consequently, it is not difficult to conceive the status of the un-witnessed in the context of a datum which must be essentially considered as lacunary. All that is required in order to re-insert this type of occurrence within the correlationist framework is to introduce a counter-factual such as the following: *had there been a witness*, then this occurrence would have been perceived in such and such a fashion. This counterfactual works just as well for the falling of a vase in an empty house as for a cosmic or ancestral event, however far removed. In either case, correlationism simply says the same thing as science: had there been a witness to the fall of the vase, she would have seen it fall according to the laws of gravity; had there been a witness to the emergence of life, its observation – granted the biological hypotheses about the origin of life – would have tallied with our theories about it, etc.

'Accordingly, the ancestral phenomenon in no way constitutes a new objection against correlationism – it merely dresses up an old argument; one that is as well worn as it is harmless.'

The entire basis for this rejoinder consists in conflating two distinct notions: that of the *ancestral*, and that of the (spatially) *distant* or (temporally) *ancient*.

The objection against idealism based on the distal occurrence is in fact identical with the one based on the ancient occurrence, and both are equivalent versions (temporal or spatial) of what could be called 'the objection from the un-witnessed', or from the 'un-perceived'. And the correlationist is certainly right about one thing – that the argument from the un-perceived is in fact trivial and poses no threat to correlationism. But the argument from the arche-fossil is in no way equivalent to such an objection, because the ancestral does *not* designate an ancient event – it designates an event *anterior* to terrestrial life and *hence anterior to givenness itself*. Though ancestrality is a temporal notion, its definition does not invoke distance in time, but rather anteriority in time. This is why the arche-fossil does not merely refer to an un-witnessed occurrence, but to a non-given occurrence – ancestral reality does not refer to occurrences which a lacunary givenness cannot apprehend, but to occurrences which are not contemporaneous with any givenness, whether lacunary or not. Therein lies its singularity and its critical potency with regard to correlationism.

Let us be perfectly clear on this point. The reason why the traditional objection from the un-witnessed occurrence – it being a matter of indifference whether the latter is spatial or temporal – poses no danger to correlationism is because this objection bears upon an event occurring when *there is already* givenness. Indeed, this is precisely why the objection can be spatial as well as temporal. For when I speak of an event that is distant in space, this event cannot but be contemporaneous with the consciousness presently envisaging it. Consequently, an objection bearing on something that is unperceived in space necessarily invokes an event and a consciousness which are considered as synchronic. This is why the event that is un-witnessed in space is essentially recuperable as one mode of lacunary givenness among others – it is recuperable as an in-apparent given which does not endanger the logic of correlation.

But the ancestral does not designate an absence *in* the given, and *for* givenness, but rather an absence *of* givenness as such. And this is precisely what the example of the spatially unperceived remains incapable of capturing – only a specific type of *temporal* reality is capable of capturing it; one which is not ancient in any vague sense, nor some sort of lacuna in that which is temporally given, but which must rather be identified with that which is *prior to givenness in its entirety*. It is not the world such as givenness deploys its lacunary presentation, but the world as it deploys itself when nothing is given, whether fully or lacunarily. Once this has been acknowledged, then one must concede that the ancestral poses a challenge to correlationism which is of an entirely different order than that of the unperceived, viz., *how to conceive of a time in which the given as such passes from non-being into being*?. Not a time which is given in a lacunary fashion, but a time wherein one passes from the lacuna of all givenness to the effectivity of a lacunary givenness.

Accordingly, there can be no question of resolving this problem by invoking a counterfactual, since this would presuppose precisely what is being called into question: if a consciousness had observed the emergence of terrestrial life, the time of the emergence *of* the given would have been a time of emergence *in* the given. But the time at issue here is the time wherein *consciousness* as well as *conscious time* have *themselves emerged in time*. For the problem of the arche-fossil is not the empirical problem of the birth of living organisms, but the ontological problem of the coming into being of givenness as such. More acutely, the problem consists in understanding how science is able to think – without any particular difficulty – the coming into being of consciousness and its spatio-temporal forms of givenness in the midst of a space and time which are supposed to pre-exist the latter. More particularly, one thereby begins to grasp that science thinks a time in which the passage from the non-being of givenness to its being has effectively occurred – hence *a time which, by definition, cannot be reduced to any givenness which preceded it and whose emergence it allows*. In other words, at issue here is not the time of consciousness but the time of science – the time which, in order to be apprehended, must be understood as harbouring the capacity to engender not only physical things, but also correlations between given things and the giving of those things. Is this not precisely what science thinks? A time that is not only anterior to givenness, but essentially indifferent to the latter because givenness could just as well *never* have emerged if life had not arisen? Science reveals a time that not only does not need conscious time but that allows the latter to arise at a determinate point in its own flux. To think science is to think the status of a becoming which cannot be correlational because the correlate is in it, rather than it being in the correlate. So the challenge is therefore the following: to understand how *science can think a world wherein spatio-temporal givenness itself came into being within a time and a space which preceded every variety of givenness*.[12]

We now see that the sophistical nature of this first rejoinder consists in trying to occlude one lacuna by another, in trying to mask the non-being of the given by a given of non-being, as though the former could be reduced to the latter. But this switching of absences, this subterfuge of lacunae, cannot disguise the fundamental difference between our two voids – and thereby the difference between the two arguments: the trivial argument from the unperceived and the valid argument from the ancestral.[13]

2) We shall formulate the second correlationist rejoinder from a transcendental perspective, which here constitutes the more incisive objection to our argumentation:

'Your objection, made in the name of the arche-fossil, evinces an elementary confusion between the empirical and the transcendental level of the problem under consideration.

'The empirical question is that of knowing how *bodies* that were organic prior to becoming conscious appeared in an environment which is itself physical. The transcendental question consists in determining how the *science* of this physical emergence of life and consciousness is possible. Now, these two levels of thought – the empirical and the transcendental – are like the two faces of a flat sheet of paper: they are absolutely inseparable but they never intersect. But your mistake consists precisely in allowing them to intersect – you have turned a structure which should have remained flat into a Möbius strip. You proceed as though the transcendental subject – which is ultimately the subject of science – was of the same nature as the physical organ which supports it – you collapse the distinction between the conscious organ which arose within nature and the subject of science which constructs the knowledge of nature. But the difference between these two is that the conscious organ *exists*;

it is an entity in the same sense as any other physical organ; whereas the transcendental subject *simply cannot be said to exist*; which is to say that the subject is not an entity, but rather a set of *conditions* rendering objective scientific knowledge of entities possible. But a condition for objective cognition cannot be treated as an object, and since only objects can be said to exist, it is necessary to insist that a condition does not exist – precisely because it conditions.

'Consequently, your conception of a "time of science", in which both bodies and the manifestation of bodies arose, is "amphibolous" – it conflates the objective being of bodies, which do in fact emerge and perish in time, with the conditions for the objective knowledge of the objective being of bodies, which have nothing to do with any sort of time. To inscribe these conditions in time is to turn them into objects and hence to anthropologize them. But one cannot reason about these conditions in the same way as one reasons about objects. The paradox you point to arises from crossing two levels of reflection which should never be allowed to cross. It suffices to abjure such crossing for the paradox to dissolve: on the side of the object, bodies are born and die; while on the other side, conditions provide the norms for knowledge of the object. But these conditions cannot be said to be born or to die – not because they are eternal, in the manner of a divine substance (which would be to think of them as an object once again, albeit a supersensible one), but simply because they cannot be situated at the same level of reflection – to do so would engender a paradox which, like that of the liar, results from a confusion between discourse and its object. Consequently, it is perfectly admissible for you to say that bodies, which provide the objective support for subjects, are born and perish in time, but you cannot say the same about the conditions which permit knowledge of such a fact. If you do, you have simply violated one of the basic requirements for the transcendental – but you have not thereby refuted it, you have simply disregarded it. Thus you cannot claim that your problem is "ontological" rather than empirical, since your problem of the arche-fossil *is* empirical, and only empirical – it pertains to objects. As for the transcendental conditions of cognition, they cannot be said to arise or to disappear – not because they are eternal but because they are "outside time" and "outside space" – they remain out of reach of the scientific discourse about objects because they provide the forms for this discourse. Every attempt to subordinate them to the science whose exercise they allow is inherently doomed to elide the very meaning of the transcendental.'

Here we have a classic defence of Kantian idealism – the charge of conflating the empirical and the transcendental – but one which, in the present case, remains entirely ineffectual.

The core of such a rejoinder consists in immunizing the conditions of knowledge from any discourse bearing on the objects of science by arguing that a transcendental condition is not an object, and hence simply does not exist. The notion of condition allows one to 'de-ontologize' the transcendental by putting it out of reach of any reflection about being. But if the transcendental philosopher wishes to play with the notion of condition in this way, she is not likely to prevail for very long. Here is why.

We are told that the transcendental does not exist because it does not exist in the way in which objects exist. Granted, but even if we concede that the transcendental subject does not exist in the way in which objects exist, one still has to say that *there is* a transcendental subject, rather than no subject. Moreover, nothing prevents us from reflecting in turn on the conditions under which there is a transcendental subject. And among these conditions we find that there can only be a transcendental subject on condition that such a subject *takes place*.

What do we mean by 'taking place'? We mean that the transcendental, insofar as it refuses all metaphysical dogmatism, remains indissociable from the notion of a *point of view*. Let us suppose a subject without any point of view on the world – such a subject would have access to the world as a totality, without anything escaping from its instantaneous inspection of objective reality. But such a subject would thereby violate the essential finitude of the transcendental subject – the world for it would no longer be a regulatory Idea of knowledge, but rather the transparent object of an immediately achieved and effective knowledge. Similarly, it would no longer be possible to ascribe sensible receptivity and its spatio-temporal form – one of the two sources of knowledge for Kant, along with the understanding – to such a subject, which would therefore be capable of totalizing the real infinity of whatever is contained in each of these forms. By the same token, since it would no longer be bound to knowledge by perceptual adumbration, and since the world for it would no longer be a horizon but rather an exhaustively known object, such a subject could no longer be conceived as a transcendental subject of the Husserlian type.

But how do notions such as finitude, receptivity, horizon, regulative Idea of knowledge, arise? They arise because, as we said above, the transcendental subject is posited as a point of view on the world, and hence as taking *place* at the heart of the world. The subject is transcendental only insofar as it is positioned *in* the world, of which it can only ever discover a finite aspect, and which it can never recollect in its totality. But if the transcendental subject is localized among the finite objects of its world in this way, this means that *it remains indissociable from its incarnation in a body*; in other words, it is indissociable from a determinate object in the world. Granted, the transcendental is the condition for knowledge of bodies, but it is necessary to add that the body is also the condition for the taking place of the transcendental. That the transcendental subject has *this* or that body is an empirical matter, but that *it has* a body is a non-empirical condition of its taking place – the body, one could say, is the 'retro-transcendental' condition for the subject of knowledge. We will invoke an established distinction here and say that a subject is *instantiated* rather than *exemplified* by a thinking body. An entity is said to be instantiated by an individual when that entity does not exist apart from its individuation; and it is said to be merely exemplified by an individual if one assumes that the entity also exists apart from its individuation. Thus, in Plato, the entity 'man' is merely exemplified by the perceptible individual man since it also exists – and exists above all – as an Idea. By way of contrast, for an empiricist, the species 'man' is instantiated by individual men because this species does not exist apart from the individuals in which it is incarnated.

But it is clear that what distinguishes transcendental idealism from speculative idealism is the fact that the former does not posit the existence of the transcendental subject apart from its bodily individuation – otherwise, it would be guilty of speculatively hypostatizing it as an ideal and absolute subject. Thus the subject is instantiated rather than exemplified by thinking bodies. But if this is so, then when we raise the question of the emergence of thinking bodies in time we are also raising the question of *the temporality of the conditions of instantiation, and hence of the taking place of the transcendental as such*. Objective bodies may not be a sufficient condition for the taking place of the transcendental, but they are certainly a necessary condition for it. We thereby discover that the time of science temporalizes and spatializes the emergence of living bodies; that is to say, *the emergence of the conditions for the taking place of the transcendental*. What effectively emerged with living bodies were the instantiations of the subject, its character as point-of-view-on-the-world. The fact that subjects emerged here on this earth or existed elsewhere is a purely empirical matter. But the fact that subjects *appeared* – simply appeared – *in* time and space, instantiated by bodies, is a matter that pertains indissociably both to objective bodies and to transcendental subjects. And we realize that this problem simply cannot be thought from the transcendental viewpoint because it concerns the space-time in which transcendental subjects went from not-taking-place to taking-place – and hence concerns the space-time anterior to the spatio-temporal forms of representation. To think this ancestral space-time is thus to think the conditions of science and also to revoke the transcendental as essentially inadequate to this task.

***

We now begin to grasp why ancestrality constitutes a *philosophical* problem, one liable to make us revise decisions often considered as infrangible since Kant. But we should state right away that it is not our aim here to resolve this problem; only to try to provide a rigorous formulation of it, and to do so in such a way that its resolution no longer seems utterly inconceivable to us.

To that end, we must once more emphasize what is truly at stake in what we shall henceforth call 'the problem of ancestrality'. Our question was the following: what are the conditions under which an ancestral statement remains meaningful? But as we have seen, this question harbours another one, which is more originary, and which delivers its veritable import, to wit: *how are we to conceive of the empirical sciences' capacity to yield knowledge of the ancestral realm?* For what is at stake here, under the cover of ancestrality, is the nature of scientific discourse, and more particularly of what characterizes this discourse, i.e. its *mathematical* form. Thus our question becomes: how is mathematical discourse able to describe a world where humanity is absent; a world crammed with things and events that are not the correlates of any manifestation; a world that is not the correlate of a relation to the world? This is the enigma which we must confront: *mathematics' ability to discourse about the great outdoors; to discourse about a past where both humanity and life are absent.* Or to say the same thing in the form of a paradox (which we will call 'the paradox of the arche-fossil'): how can a being manifest being's anteriority to manifestation? What is it that permits mathematical discourse to bring to light experiments whose material informs us about a world anterior to experience? We do not deny that this paradox has the appearance of a sheer contradiction – the redoubtable problem posed to us by the arche-fossil consists precisely in holding fast to this contradiction the better eventually to expose its illusory character. In order to think science's ancestral reach, we must explain why this contradiction is merely apparent.

Accordingly, we can reformulate our question thus: what is the condition that legitimates science's ancestral statements? This is a question that seems to be of the transcendental type, but it is peculiar in that its primary condition is the relinquishing of transcendentalism. It demands of us that we remain as distant from naïve realism as from correlationist subtlety, which are the two ways of refusing to see ancestrality as a problem. We must bear in mind the apparently unanswerable force of the correlationist circle (contrary to the naïve realist), as well as its irremediable incompatibility with ancestrality (contrary to the correlationist). Ultimately then, we must understand that what distinguishes the philosopher from the non-philosopher in this matter is that only the former is capable of being astonished (in the strong sense) by the straightforwardly literal meaning of the ancestral statement. The virtue of transcendentalism does not lie in rendering realism illusory, but in rendering it astonishing, i.e. apparently unthinkable, yet true, and hence eminently problematic.

The arche-fossil enjoins us to *track* thought by inviting us to discover the 'hidden passage' trodden by the latter in order to achieve what modern philosophy has been telling us for the past two centuries is impossibility itself: *to get out of ourselves*, to grasp the in-itself, to know what is whether we are or not.

Chapter 2
Metaphysics, Fideism, Speculation

To think ancestrality is to think a world without thought – a world without the givenness of the world. It is therefore incumbent upon us to break with the ontological requisite of the moderns, according to which *to be is to be a correlate*. Our task, by way of contrast, consists in trying to understand how thought is able to access the uncorrelated, which is to say, a world capable of subsisting without being given. But to say this is just to say that we must grasp how thought is able to access *an absolute*, i.e. a being whose *severance* (the original meaning of *absolutus*) and whose separateness from thought is such that it presents itself to us as non-relative to us, and hence as capable of existing whether we exist or not. But this entails a rather remarkable consequence: to think ancestrality requires that we take up once more the thought of the absolute; yet through ancestrality, it is the discourse of empirical science as such that we are attempting to understand and to legitimate. Consequently, it becomes necessary to insist that, far from encouraging us to renounce the kind of philosophy that claims to be able to discover absolute truth solely through its own resources, and far from commanding us – as the various forms of positivism would wish – *to renounce the quest for the absolute, it is science itself that enjoins us to discover the source of its own absoluteness*. For if I cannot think anything that is absolute, I cannot make sense of ancestrality, and consequently I cannot make sense of the science that allows me to know ancestrality.

Accordingly, we must take up once more the injunction to know the absolute, and break with the transcendental tradition that rules out its possibility. Is this to say that we must once again become pre-critical philosophers, or that we must go back to dogmatism? The whole problem is that such a return strikes us as strictly *impossible* – we cannot go back to being metaphysicians, just as we cannot go back to being dogmatists. On this point, we cannot but be heirs of Kantianism. Yet it seemed that we were defending a Cartesian (and hence dogmatic) thesis – viz., the distinction between primary and secondary qualities – against its critical disqualification. However, this defence – and here lies the rub – can no longer be sustained by Cartesian argumentation. The latter, it seems, has become irrevocably obsolete. So we must begin by trying to understand the underlying reason for this obsolescence – for as we shall see, it is by grasping the reason for this inadequacy of Cartesianism that we will be able, through the same movement, to conceive of the possibility of another relation to the absolute.

***

How does Descartes justify the thesis of the absolute existence of extended substance – and hence of the non-correlational reach of the mathematical discourse about bodies? His reasoning can be briefly recapitulated as follows:

1. I can prove the existence of a perfect, all-powerful God.
   We know that one of the three proofs for the existence of God put forward by Descartes in his *Meditations* is one that, since Kant, has come to be known as 'the ontological proof' (or argument). It proceeds by inferring God's existence from his definition as an infinitely perfect being – since He is posited as perfect, and since existence is a perfection, God cannot but exist. Since he conceives of God as existing necessarily, whether I exist to think of Him or not, Descartes assures me of a possible access to an absolute reality – a Great Outdoors that is not a correlate of my thought.
2. Since this God is perfect, He cannot deceive me when I make proper use of my understanding; that is to say, when I reason through clear and distinct ideas.
3. It seems to me that there exist outside me bodies of which I possess a distinct idea when I attribute to them nothing but three-dimensional extension. Consequently, the latter must effectively exist outside me, for otherwise God would be deceitful, which is contrary to His nature.[1]

If we consider the nature of the procedure followed by Descartes, independently of its content, we see that the argument proceeds as follows.

1. It establishes the existence of an absolute – a perfect God (or what we will call a 'primary absolute'). 2. It derives from this primary absolute the absolute reach of mathematics (or what we will call a 'derivative absolute') by emphasizing that a perfect God would not deceive us. By 'absolute reach' we mean that any aspect of a body that can be thought mathematically (whether through arithmetic or geometry) can exist absolutely outside me. However, if we consider the form which our argument should take, we cannot see any other way of absolutizing mathematical discourse other than by accessing an absolute which, even if it is not itself immediately mathematical (e.g. the perfect God), must prove subsequently capable of allowing us to derive the absoluteness of mathematics (e.g. the truthful God who ensures the existence of extended bodies). We shall therefore have to strive to provide an argument conforming to the same structure. But in order to bring out the content of our own argument, we must begin by explaining in what regard the content of the Cartesian argument is incapable of withstanding the correlationist critique.

How would a correlationist refute the preceding argument? There are in fact (at least) two ways of refuting it, depending on the *model* of correlationism which one adopts. We can effectively distinguish between two types of correlationism: a 'weak' model, which is that of Kant, and a 'strong' model, which seems to be dominant today, even if it is never explicitly thematized as such. We shall begin by expounding the refutation of the ontological argument according to the weak model – i.e. Kant's refutation – then go on to show why this model itself remains vulnerable to criticism from the perspective of an even stricter form of correlationism. We shall then see why the 'strong' model proposes the most radical refutation of any attempt to think an absolute.

It would seem, in light of what we have said so far, that it is easy to criticize Descartes. All one has to do is apply the argument of the 'correlationist circle' to Descartes' ontological proof. One would then say the following: 'Descartes' proof is fallacious at its very root, precisely insofar as it is intended to access an absolute existence. For its inference, according to which if God is perfect, then he must exist, claims to be a necessary one. But even if we were to grant that this necessity is not merely sophistical, it still would not have proven the existence of an absolute, because the necessity it affirms is merely a necessity *for us*. But we have no grounds for maintaining that this necessity, which is for us, is also a necessity in itself – we can reiterate the argument from hyperbolic doubt and maintain that we cannot know for sure that our minds are not originally deluded, leading us to believe in the truth of an argument which is actually inconsequential. Or to put it more straightforwardly: because absolute necessity is always absolute necessity for us, necessity is never absolute, but only ever for us.'

Thus, the correlationist circle proceeds by unmasking the vicious circularity inherent in every attempt at absolutization, without regard for the substance of the arguments put forward. There is no need to examine Descartes' proof, since the nub of the refutation pertains to the pretension to be able to think the absolute, rather than to any of the details deployed to that end.

Yet as we know, this is not how Kant himself refutes the ontological proof in the Transcendental Dialectic of the *Critique of Pure Reason*. For Kant in fact proposes a detailed refutation of Descartes' own argument, exposing its sophistical character. Why then is Kant not content with using an argument like the one above?

The nub of the Cartesian argument lies in the idea that the notion of a non-existent God is inherently *contradictory*. For Descartes, to think God as non-existent is to think a predicate that contradicts its subject, like a triangle that does not have three angles. Existence belongs to the very definition of God, just as the triad of angles belongs to the very definition of triangle. But in order to disqualify this argument, it is imperative for Kant to demonstrate that there is in fact no contradiction involved in maintaining that God does not exist. For if there was, it would be necessary to concede that Descartes has effectively attained an absolute. Why? Because although the author of the *Critique of Pure Reason* maintains that the thing-in-itself is unknowable, he also maintains that it is *thinkable*. For Kant effectively allows us the possibility of knowing *a priori* that logical contradiction is *absolutely* impossible. Although we cannot apply categorial cognition to the thing-in-itself, the latter remains subject to the logical condition that is the prerequisite for all thought. Consequently, for Kant, the following two propositions have an absolute ontological scope:

1. The thing-in-itself is non-contradictory.
2. The thing-in-itself exists, otherwise there would be appearances without anything that appears, which for Kant is contradictory.[2]

This is why it is imperative for Kant that Descartes' thesis be refuted – for if it was contradictory for God not to exist, then by Kant's own premises, it would also be absolutely necessary (and not just necessary for us) that God exist. Consequently, it would become possible to obtain positive knowledge of the thing-in-itself through the use of a logical principle alone. What principle underlies Kant's critique of Descartes? As we know, this critique proceeds by denying that contradiction can obtain anywhere except between an already existing entity and one of its predicates. If we assume that a triangle exists, we cannot, on pain of contradiction, attribute to it more or less than three angles. But if we reject this triangle, which is to say, 'if we reject subject and predicate alike, there is no contradiction, for nothing is then left that can be contradicted.'[3] Thus, the subject of a proposition can never impose its existence upon thought solely by virtue of its concept, for being is never part of the concept of the subject, it is never its predicate – it is added to this concept as a pure positing. Although one may maintain that a perfect being should possess existence, one cannot maintain that our conceiving of it as perfect entails its existence. There is no such 'prodigious predicate', we might say, capable of conferring *a priori* existence upon its recipient. In other words, Kant – following Hume – disqualifies the ontological proof on the grounds that there is no contradiction involved in conceiving of a determinate entity as existing or not existing. No determination of an entity can tell us *a priori* whether this entity exists or not – if we mean anything at all by the predicate 'infinitely perfect', we cannot infer from it the existence of its subject; and if we do infer its existence, this is because we are no longer saying anything meaningful in using this predicate.

As we know, this Kantian refutation of the ontological argument has implications extending well beyond its specific critique of the Cartesian proof, for it is not just a matter of rejecting the proof of God's existence, but of refuting every proof that would presume to demonstrate the absolute necessity of a determinate entity. We will call 'real necessity' this ontological register of necessity which states that such and such an entity (or determinate *res*) necessarily exists. And it would seem that this type of necessity can be found in all the variants of dogmatic metaphysics. For to be dogmatic is invariably to maintain that this or that – i.e. some determinate entity – must absolutely be, and be the way it is, whether it is Idea, pure Act, atom, indivisible soul, harmonious world, perfect God, infinite substance, World-Soul, global history, etc. But if we characterize a metaphysics minimally in terms of this kind of claim, viz., that such and such an entity must absolutely be, we then begin to understand how metaphysics culminates in the ontological argument, viz., in the claim that this or that entity must absolutely be *because* it is the way it is. The ontological argument posits a necessary being 'par excellence' insofar as the essence of this being provides the reason for its existence – it is because God's essence is to be perfect that He must necessarily exist.

But we also begin to understand how this proof is intrinsically tied to the culmination of a principle first formulated by Leibniz, although already at work in Descartes, viz., *the principle of sufficient reason*, according to which for every thing, every fact, and every occurrence, there must be a reason why it is thus and so rather than otherwise.[4] For not only does such a principle require that there be a possible explanation for every worldly fact; it also requires that thought account for the unconditioned totality of beings, as well as for their being thus and so. Consequently, although thought may well be able to account for the facts of the world by invoking this or that global law – nevertheless, it must also, according to the principle of reason, account for why these laws are thus and not otherwise, and therefore account for why the world is thus and not otherwise. And even were such a 'reason for the world' to be furnished, it would yet be necessary to account for this reason, and so on *ad infinitum.* If thought is to avoid an infinite regress while submitting to the principle of reason, it is incumbent upon it to uncover a reason that would prove capable of accounting for everything, including itself – a reason not conditioned by any other reason, and which only the ontological argument is capable of uncovering, since the latter secures the existence of an X through the determination of this X alone, rather than through the determination of some entity other than X – X must be because it is perfect, and hence *causa sui*, or sole cause of itself.

If every variant of dogmatic metaphysics is characterized by the thesis that *at least one* entity is absolutely necessary (the thesis of real necessity), it becomes clear how metaphysics culminates in the thesis according to which *every* entity is absolutely necessary (the principle of sufficient reason). Conversely, to reject dogmatic metaphysics means to reject *all* real necessity, and *a fortiori* to reject the principle of sufficient reason, as well as the ontological argument, which is the keystone that allows the system of real necessity to close in upon itself. Such a refusal enjoins us to maintain that there is no legitimate demonstration that a determinate entity should exist unconditionally. We might also add in passing that such a refusal of dogmatism furnishes the minimal condition for every critique of ideology, insofar as an ideology cannot be identified with just any variety of deceptive representation, but is rather any form of pseudo-rationality whose aim is to establish that what exists as a matter of fact exists necessarily. The critique of ideologies, which ultimately always consists in demonstrating that a social situation which is presented as inevitable is actually contingent, is essentially indissociable from the critique of metaphysics, the latter being understood as the illusory manufacturing of necessary entities. In this regard, we have no desire to call into question the contemporary desuetude of metaphysics. For the kind of dogmatism which claims that this God, this world, this history, and ultimately this actually existing political regime necessarily exists, and must be the way it is – this kind of *absolutism* does indeed seem to pertain to an era of thinking to which it is neither possible nor desirable to return.

Accordingly, the conditions for the resolution of the problem of ancestrality become more perspicuous even as they narrow considerably. In order to preserve the meaning of ancestral statements without regressing to dogmatism, *we must uncover an absolute necessity that does not reinstate any form of absolutely necessary entity*. In other words, we must think an absolute necessity without thinking anything that *is* absolutely necessary. Let us set aside for the moment this assertion's apparently paradoxical character. The only thing we have to acknowledge for the time being is that we have little choice: if one does not accept the unconditional validity of the principle of sufficient reason, nor that of the ontological argument; and if one does not accept the correlationist interpretations of ancestral statements either, then it is precisely in the assertion above – of an absolute without an absolute entity – that we will have to look for the key to the solution.

We can put it another way. Let us call 'speculative' every type of thinking that claims to be able to access some form of absolute, and let us call 'metaphysics' every type of thinking that claims to be able to access some form of absolute being, or access the absolute through the principle of sufficient reason. If all metaphysics is 'speculative' by definition, our problem consists in demonstrating, conversely, that not all speculation is metaphysical, and not every absolute is dogmatic – it is possible to envisage an *absolutizing* thought that would not be *absolutist*. The question of ancestrality thereby finds itself fundamentally tied to the critique of what could be called the '*de-absolutizing implication*', which states that 'if metaphysics is obsolete, so is the absolute'. Only by refuting such an inference, which claims that the end of dogmatic metaphysics entails the end of every absolute, can we hope to unravel the paradox of the arche-fossil.

* * *

But first we must expound that variety of correlationism which is the most rigorous, as well as the most contemporary. For it is only by confronting the most radical form of the correlation that we will be able to know whether in fact de-absolutization is the unsurpassable horizon for all philosophy.

We claimed above that Kantian transcendentalism could be identified with a 'weak' correlationism. Why? The reason is that the Critical philosophy does not prohibit all relation between thought and the absolute. It proscribes any knowledge of the thing-in-itself (any application of the categories to the supersensible), but maintains the thinkability of the in-itself. According to Kant, we know *a priori* that the thing-in-itself is non-contradictory and that it actually exists. By way of contrast, the strong model of correlationism maintains not only that it is illegitimate to claim that we can *know* the in-itself, but *also* that it is illegitimate to claim that we can at least *think* it. The argument for this de-legitimation is very simple and familiar to everyone: it proceeds, again and always, by way of the correlationist circle. For by what miraculous operation is Kantian thought able to get out of itself in order to verify that what is unthinkable for us is impossible in itself? Even if we grant that contradiction is impossible, how can Kant know that there is no God all powerful enough to render a contradiction true, as Descartes, for example, insisted?[5] Kant believes that we are not making a cognitive claim about the thing-in-itself when we submit it to the (supposedly empty) principle of non-contradiction, as he does. But on the contrary, it seems presumptuous to believe that one is capable of penetrating so deeply into the in-itself that one is able to *know* that God's omnipotence could not extend as far as logical inconsistency. This is not to say that strong correlationism asserts the existence of such an all-powerful God, but that it is content to disqualify any attempt to refute the possibility of the latter.

Conversely, there is a 'nihilist counterpart' to the hypothesis of an all-powerful God, which could also be maintained. It would consist in upholding a thesis that rejects the *second* of Kant's absolute propositions, viz., *that there is* a thing-in-itself beyond our representations. For how would one refute *a priori* the claim that there is nothing beyond phenomena, and that our world is bounded by a nothingness into which every thing could ultimately sink? One could maintain that phenomena have no basis in things-in-themselves, and that all that exists are 'phenomenal realms', which is to say, transcendental subjects, coordinated between themselves but unfolding and 'floating' in the midst of an absolute nothingness into which everything could dissolve once more were the human species to disappear. Perhaps we might be tempted to dismiss such a hypothesis as absurd, and retort that the use of the term 'nothingness' in such a context is meaningless. Yet it is precisely such a hypothesis that is legitimate for strong correlationism – for there is no way for thought to reject the possibility that what is meaningless for us might be veridical in itself. Why should what is meaningless be impossible? As far as we know, no one has ever come back from a voyage into the in-itself with a guarantee that meaning is absolute. Moreover, statements such as 'contradiction is possible' or 'nothingness is possible' are not as meaningless as they might seem, since they can be distinguished – thus the apparently contradictory belief in a redemptive Trinity is not the same as the belief in the threat of nothingness, given the divergent attitudes to life which are likely to follow from each of these two theses. The unthinkable can be declined (in the grammatical sense), as can beliefs and mysteries.

It is this strong model of de-absolutization that we are going to have to confront, since this is the model that prohibits most decisively the possibility of thinking what there is when there is no thought. It is based upon two decisions of thought, the first of which we have already considered, while the second we have yet to examine.

The first decision is that of all correlationism – it is the thesis of the essential inseparability of the act of thinking from its content. All we ever engage with is what is given-to-thought, never an entity subsisting by itself.

This decision alone suffices to disqualify every absolute of the *realist* or *materialist* variety. Every materialism that would be speculative, and hence for which absolute reality is an *entity without thought*, must assert *both* that thought is not necessary (something can be independently of thought), and that thought can think what there must be when there is no thought. The materialism that chooses to follow the speculative path is thereby constrained to believe that it is possible to think a given reality by abstracting from the fact that we are thinking it. Such is the case with Epicureanism, the paradigm of all materialism, which claims that thought can access the absolute nature of all things through the notions of atoms and void, and which asserts that this nature is not necessarily correlated with an act of thought, since thought exists only in an aleatory manner, being immanent to contingent atomic compounds (for the gods themselves are decomposable), which are in-essential for the existence of elementary natures.[6] By way of contrast, the correlationist perspective insists that it is impossible to abstract from the real the fact that it is always-already *given* to an entity, and that since it is not possible to think anything that would not always-already be given-to, we cannot think a world without an entity capable of receiving this givenness; that is to say, without an entity capable of 'thinking' this world in the most general sense, i.e. intuiting it and discoursing about it. We will refer to this first decision of strong correlationism as that of 'the primacy of the unseparated' or 'the primacy of the correlate'.

The second decision of strong correlationism will occupy us a little longer. For strong correlationism must ward off a second kind of absolute; one that is more redoubtable than the preceding variety because it seems to be more consistent. This second metaphysical strategy, which we evoked very briefly in Chapter 1, consists in *absolutizing the correlation itself*. Its basic line of argument may be summarized as follows: it was claimed that the Kantian notion of the thing-in-itself was not only unknowable, but also unthinkable. But if so, then it seems that the wisest course is simply to *abolish* any such notion of the in-itself. Accordingly, it will be maintained that the notion of the in-itself is devoid of truth because it is unthinkable, and that it should be abolished so that only the relation between subject and object remains, or some other correlation deemed to be more fundamental. A metaphysics of this type may select from among various forms of subjectivity, but it is invariably characterized by the fact that it hypostatizes some mental, sentient, or vital term: representation in the Leibnizian monad; Schelling's Nature, or the objective subject-object; Hegelian Mind; Schopenhauer's Will; the Will (or *Wills*) to Power in Nietzsche; perception loaded with memory in Bergson; Deleuze's Life, etc. Even in those cases where the vitalist hypostatization of the correlation (as in Nietzsche or Deleuze) is explicitly identified with a critique of 'the subject' or of 'metaphysics', it shares with speculative idealism the same twofold decision which ensures its irreducibility to naïve realism or some variant of transcendental idealism:

1. Nothing can be unless it is some form of relation-to-the-world (consequently, the Epicurean atom, which has neither intelligence, nor will, nor life, is impossible).
2. The previous proposition must be understood in an absolute sense, rather than as merely relative to our knowledge.

The primacy of the unseparated has become so powerful that in the modern era, even speculative materialism seems to have been dominated by these anti-rationalist doctrines of life and will, to the detriment of a 'materialism of matter' which takes seriously the possibility that there is nothing living or willing in the inorganic realm. Thus, the rivalry between the metaphysics of Life and the metaphysics of Mind masks an underlying agreement which both have inherited from transcendentalism – anything that is totally a-subjective cannot be.

Let us continue our analysis of this model. If strong correlationism can easily rebuff the realist who figures as its 'external' adversary, it is altogether more difficult for it to defeat the 'subjectivist' metaphysician who is its 'internal' adversary. For how is one to legitimate the assertion that something subsists beyond our representations when one has already insisted that this beyond is radically inaccessible to thought? It is at this stage that strong correlationism's second decision intervenes – a decision that no longer pertains to the correlation, but rather to the facticity of the correlation. Let us go back to Kant. What is it that distinguishes the Kantian project – that of transcendental idealism – from the Hegelian project – that of speculative idealism? The most decisive difference seems to be the following: Kant maintains that we can only *describe* the *a priori* forms of knowledge (space and time as forms of intuition and the twelve categories of the understanding), whereas Hegel insists that it is possible to *deduce* them. Unlike Hegel then, Kant maintains that it is impossible to derive the forms of thought from a principle or system capable of endowing them with absolute necessity. These forms constitute a 'primary fact' which is only susceptible to description, and not to deduction (in the genetic sense). And if the realm of the in-itself can be distinguished from the phenomenon, this is precisely because of the facticity of these forms, the fact that they can only be described, for if they were deducible, as is the case with Hegel, theirs would be an unconditional necessity that abolishes the possibility of there being an in-itself that could differ from them.

Thus absolute idealism and strong correlationism share an identical starting point – that of the unthinkability of the in-itself – but then go on to draw two opposite conclusions from it – that the absolute is thinkable, or that it is unthinkable, respectively. It is the irremediable facticity of the correlational forms which allows us to distinguish both claims in favour of the latter. For once one has refused any possibility of demonstrating the absolute necessity of these forms, it is impossible to proscribe the possibility that there could be an in-itself that differs fundamentally from what is given to us. Like Kantianism, strong correlationism insists upon the facticity of these forms, but differs from the former by extending this facticity to logical form as well – which is to say, to the principle of non-contradiction, for just as we can only describe the *a priori* forms of sensibility and the understanding, similarly, we can only describe the logical principles inherent in every thinkable proposition, but we cannot deduce their absolute truth. Consequently, there is no sense in claiming to know that contradiction is absolutely impossible, for the only thing that is given to us is the fact that we cannot think anything that is self-contradictory.

Let us try to attain a better grasp of the nature of this facticity, since its role in the process of de-absolutization seems to be just as fundamental as that of the correlation. First of all, from the perspective of the strong model, it is essential to distinguish this facticity from the mere perishability of worldly entities. In fact, the facticity of forms has nothing to do with the destructability of a material object, or with vital degeneration. When I maintain that this or that entity or event is contingent, I know something positive about them – I know that this house can be destroyed, I know that it would have been physically possible for this person to act differently, etc. *Contingency* expresses the fact that physical laws remain indifferent as to whether an event occurs or not – they allow an entity to emerge, to subsist, or to perish. But *facticity*, by way of contrast, pertains to those structural invariants that supposedly govern the world – invariants which may differ from one variant of correlationism to another, but whose function in every case is to provide the minimal organization of representation: principle of causality, forms of perception, logical laws, etc. These structures are fixed – I never experience their variation, and in the case of logical laws, I cannot even represent to myself their modification (thus for example, I cannot represent to myself a being that is contradictory or non self-identical). But although these forms are fixed, they constitute a fact, rather than an absolute, since I cannot ground their necessity – their facticity reveals itself with the realization that they can only be described, not founded. But this is a fact that – contrary to those merely empirical facts whose being-otherwise I can experience – does not provide me with any positive knowledge. For if contingency consists in knowing that worldly things could be otherwise, facticity just consists in not knowing why the correlational structure has to be thus. This is a point that should be borne in mind throughout what follows: in insisting upon the facticity of correlational forms, the correlationist is *not* saying that these forms could actually change; he is merely claiming that we cannot think why it should be impossible for them to change, nor why a reality wholly other than the one that is given to us should be proscribed *a priori*. Consequently, we must distinguish between:

1. The intra-worldly contingency which is predicated of everything that can be or not be, occur or not occur, within the world without contravening the invariants of language and representation through which the world is given to us.
2. The facticity of these invariants as such, which is a function of our inability to establish either their necessity *or* their contingency.

What I experience with facticity is not an objective reality, but rather the unsurpassable limits of objectivity confronted with the fact *that there is* a world; a world that is describable and perceptible, and structured by determinate invariants. It is the sheer fact of the world's logicality, of its givenness in a representation, which evades the structures of logical and representational reason. The in-itself becomes opaque to the point where it is no longer possible to maintain that it exists, so that the term tends to disappear to the benefit of facticity alone.

Facticity thereby forces us to grasp the 'possibility' of that which is wholly other to the world, but which resides in the midst of the world as such. Yet it is necessary to place inverted commas around the term 'possibility' insofar as what is operative in facticity is not knowledge of the actual possibility of the wholly other, but rather our inability to establish its impossibility. It is a possibility which is itself hypothetical, indicating that for us every hypothesis concerning the in-itself remains equally valid – that it is, that it is necessary, that it is not, that it is contingent, etc. Thus this 'possibility' does not amount to any sort of positive knowledge of this wholly other; not even the positive knowledge that there is, or could be something wholly other – it is just the mark of our essential *finitude*, as well as of the world itself (even if the latter has no physical limits). For facticity fringes both knowledge and the world with an absence of foundation whose converse is that nothing can be said to be absolutely impossible, not even the unthinkable. In other words, facticity pushes the critique of the principle of sufficient reason to its ultimate extreme, by pointing out not only that the ontological argument is illegitimate, but also that the principle of non-contradiction itself is without reason, and that consequently it can only be the norm for what is thinkable by us, rather than for what is possible in an absolute sense. Facticity is the 'un-reason' (the absence of reason) of the given as well as of its invariants.

Thus the strong model of correlationism can be summed up in the following thesis: *it is unthinkable that the unthinkable be impossible*. I cannot provide a rational ground for the absolute impossibility of a contradictory reality, or for the nothingness of all things, even if the meaning of these terms remains indeterminate. Accordingly, facticity entails a specific and rather remarkable consequence: it becomes rationally illegitimate to disqualify *irrational* discourses about the absolute on the pretext of their irrationality. From the perspective of the strong model, in effect, religious belief has every right to maintain that the world was created out of nothingness from an act of love, or that God's omnipotence allows him to dissolve the apparent contradiction between his complete identity and His difference with his Son. These discourses continue to be meaningful – in a mythological or mystical register – even though they are scientifically and logically meaningless. Consequently, the most general thesis of the strong model pertains to the existence of a regime of meaning that remains incommensurable with rational meaning because it does not pertain to the facts of the world, but rather to the very fact that there is a world. Yet correlationism itself does not maintain *any* irrational position, whether religious or poetic; it makes no positive pronouncements whatsoever about the absolute; rather it confines itself to thinking the limits of thought, these functioning for language like a frontier only one side of which can be grasped. Thus, correlationism provides no positive ground for any specific variety of religious belief, but it undermines reason's claim to be able to disqualify a belief on the grounds that its content is unthinkable.

The strong model in this characterization seems to us to be represented as much by Wittgenstein as by Heidegger, which is to say, by the two emblematic representatives of the two principal currents of twentieth-century philosophy: analytic philosophy and phenomenology. Thus, the *Tractatus* maintains that the logical form of the world cannot be stated in the way in which facts in the world can be; it can only be 'shown', that is to say, indicated in accordance with a discursive register that cannot be bound by the categories of science or logic. Consequently, it is the very fact that the world is sayable (that is to say, liable to formulation according to a logical syntax) that cannot be bound by logical discourse. Whence proposition 6.522: 'There are indeed things that cannot be put into words. They *make themselves manifest*. They are what is mystical.'[7]

But the mystical does not consist in other-worldly knowledge – it is the indication of science's inability to think the fact *that there is* a world. Hence proposition 6.44: 'It is not *how* things are in the world that is mystical, but *that* it exists.'[8] Similarly, we have already seen how for Heidegger it is the very fact that there are beings, and that there is a givenness of beings, that points to the rift inherent in representation: 'Of all beings, only the human being, called upon by the voice of Being, experiences the wonder of all wonders: *that* beings *are*.'[9] In both cases, the fact that beings are, or the fact that there is a logical world, is precisely what cannot be encompassed by the sovereignty of logic and metaphysical reason, and this because of the facticity of the 'there is'; a facticity which can certainly be thought – since it is not grasped through a transcendent revelation, but merely through a grasp of the 'internal limits' of this world – but thought solely on account of our inability to gain access to the absolute ground of what is. I cannot think the unthinkable, but I can think that it is not impossible for the impossible to be.

In summary: where the weak model of correlationism de-absolutized the principle of sufficient reason by disqualifying every proof of unconditional necessity, the strong model pushes this disqualification of the principle of sufficient reason still further, and de-absolutizes the principle of non-contradiction by re-inscribing every representation within the bounds of the correlationist circle.[10] We have now identified the two operations that underlie the contemporary justification for the renunciation of the absolute – not only that of the primacy of the correlation against every form of 'naïve realism', but also that of the facticity of the correlation against every form of 'speculative idealism'.[11]

However, two fundamental types of strong correlationism can be envisaged, each crystallizing and opposing the other around the following question: does the de-absolutization of thought also imply the *de-universalization* of thought? Those philosophers who respond to this question in the negative will situate themselves as heirs of Kant's critical legacy and will attempt, in the wake of Kant, to uncover the universal conditions for our relation to the world, whether these be construed as conditions for empirical science, conditions for linguistic communication between individuals, conditions for the perceptibility of the entity, etc. But even a 'strong' correlationist who claims to remain faithful to the spirit of the Critical philosophy will not allow herself to justify the universality of non-contradiction by invoking its putative absoluteness – rather than characterizing the former as a property of the thing-in-itself, she will construe it as a universal condition for the sayability of the given, or for intersubjective communication – it will be a norm of the thinkable, not of the possible.[12] Contrarily, those philosophers, such as the partisans of 'radical finitude' or of 'postmodernity', who dismiss every variety of universal as a mystificatory relic of the old metaphysics will claim that it is necessary to think the facticity of our relation to the world in terms of a *situation that is itself finite*, and hence modifiable by right; a situation which it would be illusory to think we could gain enough distance from to formulate statements that would be valid for all humans, in all times and all places. Accordingly, the correlations which determine 'our' world will be identified with a situation anchored in a determinate era of the history of being, or in a form of life harbouring its own language-games, or in a determinate cultural and interpretative community, etc.

The only remaining legitimate question for both parties is the following: should this limitation of our knowing to our relation to the world extend so far as to disqualify the possibility of maintaining a universal discourse concerning the very nature of this relation? Both parties will concur regarding the desuetude of unconditional necessity, so that the sole remaining question will concern the status of the correlation's conditional necessity; that is to say, the status of the conditions of possibility of language and the given. The metaphysical statement 'if an entity is thus, it must absolutely be' gives way to the post-metaphysical statement 'if an entity gives itself immediately as thus (as perceptible, sayable, etc.), it will have as its more general (i.e. deeper, more originary) condition to be thus (to be given by adumbrations, to be non-contradictory, etc.)'. It is no longer a matter of 'X is thus, therefore X must be', but 'if as a matter of fact X is given as thus, then it has as its condition to be thus'. The debate will be about the determination of these conditions, i.e. about whether or not there are universal conditions of language and the given.

Strong correlationism is not always thematized as such by those who espouse it – yet its contemporary predominance seems to us to be intimately connected to the immunity from the constraints of conceptual rationality which religious belief currently seems to enjoy. What philosopher nowadays would claim to have refuted the possibility of the Christian Trinity on the grounds that he had detected a contradiction in it? Wouldn't a philosopher who dismissed Levinas' thought of the 'wholly Other' as absurd on the grounds that it is refractory to logic be derided as a dusty freethinker, incapable of rising to the heights of Levinas' discourse? It is important to understand what underlies this attitude: religious belief is considered to be beyond the reach of rational refutation by many contemporary philosophers not only because such belief is deemed by definition indifferent to this kind of critique, but because it seems to these philosophers to be *conceptually* illegitimate to undertake such a refutation. A Kantian who believed in the Trinity would have been obliged to demonstrate that the idea of the latter is not self-contradictory, but a strong correlationist only has to demonstrate that reason has no right to deploy its own resources to debate the truth or falsity of this dogma. It should be underlined that this gap that separates contemporary philosophers from the Kantian position is far from innocuous. It points to a major shift that has occurred in our conception of thought from Kant's time to ours. This shift, from the unknowability of the thing-in-itself to its unthinkability, indicates that thought has reached the stage where it legitimates *by its own development* the fact that being has become so opaque for it that thought supposes the latter to be capable of transgressing the most elementary principles of the *logos*. Where the Parmenidean postulate, 'being and thinking are the same', remained the prescription for all philosophy up to and including Kant, it seems that the fundamental postulate of strong correlationism can be formulated thus: '*being and thinking must be thought as capable of being wholly other*'. Again, this is not to say that the correlationist believes herself to be in a position to declare the fundamental incommensurability between thought and being, such as by declaring the actual existence of a God incommensurable with all conceptualization, since this would assume a knowledge of the in-itself which she has completely abjured. But she sees herself as at least able to emphasize a facticity of the thought-being correlation so radical that it deprives her of any right to rule out the possibility of there being no common measure between the in-itself and what thought can conceive. This radicalization of the correlation has given rise to what we might call a '*possible whole alteration*' of thought and being. The unthinkable can only draw us back to our inability to think otherwise, rather than to the absolute impossibility of things being wholly otherwise.

It then becomes clear that this trajectory culminates in the disappearance of the pretension to *think* any absolutes, *but not in the disappearance of absolutes*; since in discovering itself to be marked by an irremediable limitation, correlational reason thereby legitimates *all* those discourses that claim to access an absolute, *the only proviso being that nothing in these discourses resembles a rational justification of their validity*. Far from abolishing the value of the absolute, the process that continues to be referred to today as 'the end of absolutes' grants the latter an unprecedented licence – philosophers seem to ask only one thing of these absolutes: that they be devoid of the slightest pretension to rationality. The end of metaphysics, understood as the 'de-absolutization of thought', is thereby seen to consist in the rational legitimation of any and every variety of religious (or 'poetico-religious') belief in the absolute, so long the latter invokes no authority beside itself. To put it in other words: *by forbidding reason any claim to the absolute, the end of metaphysics has taken the form of an exacerbated return of the religious*. Or again: the end of ideologies has taken the form of the unqualified victory of religiosity. There are certainly historical reasons for the contemporary resurgence of religiosity, which it would be naïve to reduce to developments in philosophy alone; but the fact that thought, under the pressure of correlationism, has relinquished its right to criticize the irrational when the latter lays claim to the absolute, should not be underestimated when considering the extent of this phenomenon.

Yet even today, this 'return of the religious' continues to be misunderstood on account of a powerful historical tropism, from which we must extract ourselves once and for all. This tropism, this conceptual blindness, can be described as follows. There are many who continue to believe that every critique of metaphysics 'naturally' goes hand in hand with a critique of religion. But in fact, this 'partnership between critiques' remains a function of a very specific configuration of the link between metaphysics and religion. Whenever one claims to be carrying out a critique of 'metaphysico-religious' absolutes, one has in mind the critique of onto-theology insofar as the latter coincides with the critique of Judaeo-Christian theology's claim that its belief in a unique God is founded upon supposedly rational truths, all of which are anchored in the idea of a supreme being who is the prime mover of all things. But it is necessary to point out something which, curiously enough, is not, or is no longer, self-evident. This is the fact that in criticizing metaphysics' pretension to think the absolute, we may – as indeed proved to be the case – succeed in undermining *a* particular religion which appealed to 'natural reason' in order to declare the superiority of its particular beliefs over those of other religions. Thus, for example, by destroying every form of proof for the existence of a supreme being, one removes the rational support which a specific monotheistic religion invoked against every form of polytheistic religion. Consequently, by destroying metaphysics, one has effectively rendered it impossible for a particular religion to use a pseudo-rational argumentation against every other religion. But in doing so – and this is the decisive point – one has inadvertently justified belief's claim to be the *only* means of access to the absolute. Once the absolute has become unthinkable, even atheism, which also targets God's inexistence in the manner of an absolute, is reduced to a mere belief, and hence to a religion, albeit of the nihilist kind. Faith is pitched against faith, since what determines our fundamental choices cannot be rationally proved. In other words, the de-absolutization of thought boils down to the mobilization of a *fideist* argument; but a fideism that is 'fundamenal' rather than merely 'historical' in nature – that is to say, a fideism that has become thought's defence of religiosity in general, rather than of a specific religion (as was the case in the sixteenth century with Catholic fideism, or what claimed to be such).

Fideism invariably consists in a sceptical argument directed against the pretension of metaphysics, and of reason more generally, to be able to access an absolute truth capable of shoring up (or *a fortiori*, of denigrating) the value of faith. But it is our conviction that the contemporary end of metaphysics is nothing other than the victory of such a fideism – which is actually of ancient provenance (it was initiated by the Counter-Reformation, and Montaigne is its 'founding father') – over metaphysics. Far from seeing in fideism – as is all too often the case – a mere guise worn by anti-metaphysical scepticism at its origins, before the latter went on to reveal its irreligious essence, we see scepticism as an authentic fideism, which is dominant today, but in a form that has become 'essential', which is to say, *one that has shrugged off every particular obedience to a determinate belief system.* Historical fideism is not the 'guise' that irreligiosity wore at its beginnings; rather, it is religiosity as such, which adopted the 'guise' of a specific apologia (on behalf of one religion or belief system rather than another), before revealing itself to be the general argument for the superiority of piety over thought.[13] *The contemporary end of metaphysics is an end which, being sceptical, could only be a religious end of metaphysics.*

Scepticism with regard to the metaphysical absolute thereby legitimates *de jure* every variety whatsoever of belief in an absolute, the best as well as the worst. The destruction of the metaphysical rationalization of Christian theology has resulted in a generalized becoming-religious of thought, viz., in *a fideism of any belief whatsoever.* We will call this becoming-religious of thought, which finds its paradoxical support in a radically sceptical argumentation, the *religionizing* [*enreligement*] of reason: this expression, which echoes that of rationalization, denotes a movement of thought which is the exact contrary to that of the progressive rationalization of Judaeo-Christianity under the influence of Greek philosophy. Today, everything happens as if philosophy considered itself of its own accord – rather than because of pressure exerted upon it by an external belief – to be the servant of theology – except that it now considers itself to be the liberal servant of any theology whatsoever, even an atheology. In leaving the realm of metaphysics, the absolute seems to have been fragmented into a multiplicity of beliefs that have become indifferent, all of them equally legitimate from the viewpoint of knowledge, and this simply by virtue of the fact that they themselves claim to be nothing *but* beliefs. Whence a profound transformation in the nature of incredulity, which is to say, in the nature of its argumentation. Having continuously upped the ante with scepticism and criticisms of the pretensions of metaphysics, we have ended up according all legitimacy in matters of veracity to professions of faith – and this no matter how extravagant their content. As a result, the struggle against what the Enlightenment called 'fanaticism' has been converted into a project of moralization: the condemnation of fanaticism is carried out solely in the name of its practical (ethico-political) consequences, never in the name of the ultimate falsity of its contents. On this point, the contemporary philosopher has completely capitulated to the man of faith. For thought supplies the latter with resources that support his initial decision: if there is an ultimate truth, only piety can provide it, not thought. Whence the impotence of merely moral critiques of contemporary obscurantism, for if nothing absolute is thinkable, there is no reason why the worst forms of violence could not claim to have been sanctioned by a transcendence that is only accessible to the elect few.

It is important to note that the religionizing of reason does not designate the act of faith as such – since the latter can obviously prove extremely valuable. The religionizing of reason designates the contemporary form of the *connection* between thinking and piety – and hence a movement of *thought* itself relative to piety; specifically, its *non-metaphysical subordination to the latter*. Better still: its subordination to piety via a specific mode of the destruction of metaphysics. Such is the sense of de-absolutization – thought no longer provides an *a priori* demonstration of the truth of a specific content of piety; instead, it establishes how any piety whatsoever enjoys an equal and exclusive right to grasp the ultimate truth. Contrary to the familiar view according to which Occidental modernity consists

47

in a vast enterprise of the secularization of thought, we consider the most striking feature of modernity to be the following: the modern man is he who has been re-ligionized precisely to the extent that he has been de-Christianized. The modern man is he who, even as he stripped Christianity of the ideological (metaphysical) pretension that its belief system was superior to all others, has delivered himself body and soul to the idea that all belief systems are equally legitimate in matters of veracity.

Thus, the contemporary closure of metaphysics seems to us to amount to a 'sceptico-fideist' closure of metaphysics, dominated by what one could call the thought of the 'wholly-other'. Wittgenstein and Heidegger are the emblematic representatives of this thought and, far from inaugurating a radical break with the past in this matter, both remain heirs to the legacy of a venerable and well documented fideist tradition (inaugurated by Montaigne and developed notably by Gassendi and Bayle), whose anti-metaphysical character has always been intended to protect piety from the incursions of rationality, and which reaches its culminating point in these two thinkers. The 'mystical' evoked in Wittgenstein's *Tractatus Logico-Philosophicus*, or the theology that Heidegger admitted he had long considered writing – on condition that it contained nothing philosophical, not even the word 'being'[14] – are expressions of an aspiration towards an absoluteness which would no longer retain anything metaphysical, and which one is generally careful to designate by another name. This is a piety that has been evacuated of content, and that is now celebrated for its own sake by a thinking that has given up trying to substantiate it. For the apex of fideism occurs at the point where it becomes the thought of piety's superiority to thinking, without any specific content being privileged, since it is a matter of establishing through thinking that it is the prerogative of piety, and of piety alone, to posit its own contents. Accordingly, the contemporary devolution towards the wholly-other (the otherwise empty object of the profession of faith) is the strict and inevitable obverse of interpreting the obsolescence of the principle of sufficient reason as reason's discovery of its own essential inability to uncover an absolute – thus, fideism is merely the *other name* for strong correlationism.[15]

***

We are trying to grasp the sense of the following paradox: the more thought arms itself against dogmatism, the more defenceless it becomes before fanaticism. Even as it forces metaphysical dogmatism to retreat, sceptico-fideism reinforces religious obscurantism. Now, it would be absurd to accuse all correlationists of religious fanaticism, just as it would be absurd to accuse all metaphysicians of ideological dogmatism. But it is clear to what extent the fundamental decisions that underlie metaphysics invariably reappear, albeit in a caricatural form, in ideologies (what is *must* be), and to what extent the fundamental decisions that underlie obscurantist belief may find support in the decisions of strong correlationism (it may be that the wholly-other *is*). Contemporary fanaticism cannot therefore simply be attributed to the resurgence of an archaism that is violently opposed to the achievements of Western critical reason; on the contrary, it is the *effect* of critical rationality, and this precisely insofar as – this needs to be underlined – this rationality was *effectively emancipatory;* was effectively, and thankfully, successful in destroying dogmatism. It is thanks to the critical power of correlationism that dogmatism was effectively vanquished in philosophy, and it is because of correlationism that philosophy finds itself incapable of fundamentally distinguishing itself from fanaticism. The victorious critique of ideologies has been transformed into a renewed argument for blind faith.

We thereby grasp that what is at stake in a critique of the de-absolutizing implication (viz., that if metaphysics is obsolete, so is every form of absolute) goes beyond that of the legitimation of ancestral statements. What is urgently required, in effect, is that we re-think what could be called 'the prejudices of critical-sense'; viz., critical potency is not necessarily on the side of those who would undermine the validity of absolute truths, but rather on the side of those who would succeed in criticizing *both* ideological dogmatism and sceptical fanaticism. Against dogmatism, it is important that we uphold the refusal of every metaphysical absolute, but against the reasoned violence of various fanaticisms, it is important that we re-discover in thought a modicum of absoluteness – enough of it, in any case, to counter the pretensions of those who would present themselves as its privileged trustees, solely by virtue of some revelation.

Chapter 3
The Principle of Factiality

Although not Cartesian in principle, our procedure is homologous with the one followed by Descartes in his *Meditations*, after he had successfully established the truth of the *cogito* in the second Meditation. Following Descartes' example, we are attempting to move beyond a '*cogito*' by accessing an absolute capable of founding science's (ancestral) discourse. But the *cogito* in question is no longer the Cartesian *cogito* – it is a 'correlationist *cogito*' that encloses thought in a reciprocal relation to being, one which is merely the mask for thought's underlying relation to itself. This *cogito* differs from the Cartesian *cogito* in at least two ways:

1. The correlationist *cogito* cannot necessarily be identified with a metaphysics of representation, since it can be a function of a conception of the correlation between thought and being other than the one between subject and object (e.g. Heidegger's co-propriation of man and Being).
2. It is not strictly speaking a solipsistic *cogito*, but rather a '*cogitamus*', since it founds science's objective truth upon an intersubjective consensus among consciousnesses. Yet the correlationist *cogito* also institutes a certain kind of solipsism, which could be called a 'species solipsism', or a 'solipsism of the community', since it ratifies the impossibility of thinking any reality that would be anterior or posterior to the community of thinking beings. This community only has dealings with itself, and with the world with which it is contemporaneous.

To extract ourselves from this communitarian or intersubjective solipsism is to access a great outdoors that would perform the same function for the mathematics contained in ancestral statements as the veracious God performed for extended substance.

These then are the coordinates of the problem, according to what we have established so far:

1. If the ancestral is to be thinkable, then an absolute must be thinkable.
2. We accept the disqualification of every argument intended to establish the absolute necessity of an entity – thus the absolute we seek cannot be dogmatic.
3. We must overcome the obstacle of the correlationist circle, while acknowledging that within the strong model which grants it its full extent, the latter not only disqualifies the dogmatic absolute (as did the refutation of the ontological argument), but every form of absolute in general. It is the absolutizing approach as such, and not just the absolutist one (based on the principle of sufficient reason), which seems to shatter against the obstacle presented by the vicious circle of correlation: to think something absolute is to think an absolute for-us, and hence not to think anything absolute.

What we seek then is a non-metaphysical absolute, capable of slipping through the meshes of the strong model, while acknowledging that:

– a realist absolute (e.g. Epicurean) cannot pass through the meshes of the correlation (first principle of the strong model);
– a correlationist absolute (one that is subjectivist, i.e., idealist or vitalist) cannot pass through the meshes of facticity (second principle of strong correlationism).

How then is thought to carve out a path towards the outside for itself?

***

The position of the problem, and the drastic conditions for its resolution, both indicate what appears to be the only remaining path available. In order to counter the strong model, we must take as our exemplar the first metaphysical counter-offensive against Kantian transcendentalism – in other words, we too must absolutize the very principle that allows correlationism to disqualify absolutizing thought. This is precisely what various subjectivist metaphysicians did – they turned the correlation itself, the instrument of empirico-critical de-absolutization, into the model for a new type of absolute. In doing so, these metaphysicians did not simply 'trick' correlationism; they were not trying to 'unearth' an absolute that they could then deftly turn against critico-scepticism, with the help of its own argumentation. It was more a case of trying to think the profound truth from which this argumentation derived its force. They acknowledged correlationism's discovery of a fundamental constraint – viz., that we only have access to the for-us, not the in-itself – but instead of concluding from this that the in-itself is unknowable, they concluded that the correlation is the only veritable in-itself. In so doing, they grasped the ontological truth hidden beneath the sceptical argumentation – they converted radical ignorance into knowledge of a being finally unveiled in its true absoluteness.

Yet this first wave of the counter-offensive against correlationism came to grief against the second principle of correlationism – that of the essential facticity of the correlation, which has proven to be its most profound decision – the one which disqualifies idealist as well as realist dogmatism. Accordingly, the trail we have to follow is already marked out for us – if an absolute capable of withstanding the ravages of the correlationist circle remains conceivable, it can only be the one that results from the absolutization of the strong model's second decision – *which is to say, facticity*. In other words, if we can discover an ontological truth hidden beneath facticity; if we can succeed in grasping why the very source which lends its power to the strategy of de-absolutization through fact also furnishes the means of access to an absolute being; then we will have gained access to a truth that is invulnerable to correlationist scepticism. For this time, there will be no third principle liable to counter such an absolutization. Accordingly, we must try to understand why *it is not the correlation but the facticity of the correlation that constitutes the absolute*. We must show why thought, far from experiencing its intrinsic *limits* through facticity, experiences rather its *knowledge* of the absolute through facticity. We must grasp in facticity not the inaccessibility of the absolute but the unveiling of the in-itself and the eternal property of what is, as opposed to the mark of the perennial deficiency in the thought of what is.

What could such propositions mean?

Initially, it seems absurd to think of facticity as an absolute, since the latter is supposed to express thought's inability to uncover the reason why what is, is. By turning an inability into an absolute, do we not end up with an absolute inability? The answer is no – at least not if we follow the procedure which subjectivist metaphysicians adopted with regard to the correlation. As we saw, the former uncovered the veritable instance of absolute being in the very obstacle erected against absolutization. We must now endeavour to do the same with facticity. No doubt, this will require a 'change in outlook', but once the latter has been achieved, the supreme necessity ascribed to the correlationist circle will appear as the opposite of what it first seemed – facticity will be revealed to be a knowledge of the absolute *because we are going to put back into the thing itself what we mistakenly took to be an incapacity in thought.* In other words, instead of construing the absence of reason inherent in everything as a limit that thought encounters in its search for the ultimate reason, we must understand that this absence of reason *is*, and can *only* be the *ultimate* property of the entity. We must convert facticity into the real property whereby everything and every world *is* without reason, and is thereby *capable of actually becoming otherwise without reason*. We must grasp how the ultimate absence of reason, which we will refer to as 'unreason', is an absolute ontological property, and not the mark of the finitude of our knowledge. From this perspective, the failure of the principle of reason follows, quite simply, from the *falsity* (and even from the absolute falsity) of such a principle – for the truth is that there is no reason for anything to be or to remain thus and so rather than otherwise, and this applies as much to the laws that govern the world as to the things of the world. Everything could actually collapse: from trees to stars, from stars to laws, from physical laws to logical laws; and this not by virtue of some superior law whereby everything is destined to perish, but by virtue of the absence of any superior law capable of preserving anything, no matter what, from perishing.

Let us try to be more precise about what we mean by such an absolute, and first of all, let us try to explain in what regard this absolutization of facticity is capable of overcoming the obstacle presented by the correlationist circle.

The correlationist could object to our thesis as follows: 'To claim that facticity must be understood as the knowledge of the actual absence of reason for anything is to commit an elementary mistake, for it is to conflate facticity with *contingency*. Contingency designates the possibility whereby something can either persist or perish, without either option contravening the invariants that govern the world. Thus, contingency is an instance of knowledge; the knowledge I have of the actual perish-ability of a determinate thing. I know for example that this book could be destroyed, even if I do not know when or where this destruction will occur – whether it will soon be torn up by my little girl, or rotted away decades from now by mould. But this is to know something positive about this book, viz., its actual fragility, the possibility of its not-being. However, facticity can no more be identified with contingency than with necessity, since it designates our essential ignorance about either the contingency *or* the necessity of our world and its invariants. By turning facticity into a property of things themselves – a property which I am alleged to know – I turn facticity from something that applies only to what is in the world into a form of contingency capable of being applied to the invariants that govern the world (i.e. its physical and logical laws). In so doing, I claim to know that the world is perishable, just as I know that this book is perishable. But I am no more capable of demonstrating that facticity can be equated with this contingency, considered as true in itself, than I was capable of demonstrating the existence of a supposedly necessary metaphysical principle from which our world originates. Accordingly, the correlational circle undermines the thesis of the absolute contingency of everything just as effectively as it undermined the thesis of the absolute necessity of a supreme being – for how would one know that the apparent unreason of the world is an unreason *in-itself* – i.e. the real possibility of everything's becoming other without reason – rather than just an unreason *for-us* – i.e. simply a function of our inability to discover the true necessary reason for everything, hidden behind the veil of phenomena? This movement from the *for-us* to the *in-itself* is no more acceptable in the case of contingency than it was in the case of necessity.'

There is only one way for us to counter this argument: we have to show that the correlationist circle – and what lies at the heart of it, viz., the distinction between the *in-itself* and the *for-us* – is only conceivable insofar as it already presupposes an implicit admission of the absoluteness of contingency. More precisely, we must demonstrate how the facticity of the correlation, which provides the basis for the correlationist's disquali-fication of dogmatic idealism as well as of dogmatic realism, is only conceivable on condition that one admits the absoluteness of the contin-gency of the given in general. For if we can succeed in demonstrating that the capacity-to-be-other of everything is the absolute presupposed by the circle itself, then we will have succeeded in demonstrating that one cannot de-absolutize contingency without incurring the self-destruction of the circle – which is another way of saying that contingency will turn out to have been immunized against the operation whereby correlationism relativizes the *in-itself* to the *for-us*.

We can make things clearer by considering the following example. Let us suppose that two dogmatists are arguing about the nature of our future *post-mortem*. The Christian dogmatist claims to know (because she has supposedly demonstrated it) that our existence continues after death, and that it consists in the eternal contemplation of a God whose nature is incomprehensible from within the confines of our present existence. Thus, the latter claims to have demonstrated that what is in-itself is a God who, like the Cartesian God, can be shown *by* our finite reason to be incomprehensible *for* our finite reason. But the atheist dogmatist claims to know that, on the contrary, our existence is completely abolished by death, which utterly annihilates us.

It is at this stage that the correlationist comes along to disqualify both of their positions by defending a strict theoretical agnosticism. All beliefs strike her as equally legitimate given that theory is incapable of privileging one eventuality over another. For just as I cannot know the in-itself without converting it into a for-me, I cannot know what will happen to me when I am no longer of this world, since knowledge presupposes that one is of the world. Consequently, the agnostic has little difficulty in refuting both of these positions – all she has to do is demonstrate that it is self-contradictory to claim to know what is when one is no longer alive, since knowledge presupposes that one is still of this world. Accordingly, the two dogmatists are proffering realist theses about the in-itself, both of which are vitiated by the inconsistency proper to all realism – that of claiming to think what there is when one is not.

But then another disputant intervenes: the subjective idealist. The latter declares that the position of the agnostic is every bit as inconsistent as those of the two realists. For all three believe that there could be an in-itself radically different from our present state, whether it is a God who is inaccessible to natural reason, or a sheer nothingness. But this is precisely what is unthinkable, for I am no more capable of thinking a transcendent God than the annihilation of everything – more particularly, I cannot think of myself as no longer existing without, through that very thought, contradicting myself. I can only think of myself as existing, and as existing the way I exist; thus, I cannot but exist, and always exist as I exist now. Consequently, my mind, if not my body, is immortal. Death, like every other form of radical transcendence, is annulled by the idealist, in the same way as she annuls every idea of an in-itself that differs from the correlational structure of the subject. Because an in-itself that differs from the *for-us* is unthinkable, the idealist declares it to be impossible.

The question now is under what conditions the correlationist agnostic can refute not only the theses of the two realists, but also that of the idealist. In order to counter the latter, the agnostic has no choice: she must maintain that my capacity-to-be-wholly-other in death (whether dazzled by God, or annihilated) is just as thinkable as my persisting in my self-identity. The 'reason' for this is that I think myself as devoid of any reason for being and remaining as I am, and it is the thinkability of this unreason – of this facticity – which implies that the other three theses – those of the two realists and the idealist – are all equally possible. For even if I cannot think of myself, for example, as annihilated, neither can I think of any cause that would rule out this eventuality. The possibility of my not being is thinkable as the counterpart of the absence of any reason for my being, even if I cannot think what it would be not to be. Although realists maintain the possibility of a post-mortem condition that is unthinkable as such (whether as vision of God or as sheer nothingness), the thesis they maintain is itself thinkable – for even if I cannot think the unthinkable, I can think the possibility of the unthinkable by dint of the unreason of the real. Consequently, the agnostic can recuse all three positions as instances of absolutism – all three claim to have identified a necessary reason implying one of the three states described above, whereas no such reason is available.

But now a final disputant enters the debate: the speculative philosopher. She maintains that neither the two dogmatists, nor the idealist have managed to identify the absolute, because *the latter is simply the capacity-to-be-other as such, as theorized by the agnostic*. The absolute is the *possible transition*, devoid of reason, of my state towards any other state whatsoever. But this possibility is no longer a 'possibility of ignorance'; viz., a possibility that is merely the result of my inability to know which of the three aforementioned theses is correct – rather, it is the *knowledge* of the very real possibility of all of these eventualities, as well as of a great many others. How then are we able to claim that this capacity-to-be-other is an absolute – an index of knowledge rather than of ignorance? The answer is that it is the agnostic herself who has convinced us of it. For how does the latter go about refuting the idealist? She does so by maintaining that we can *think* ourselves as no longer being; in other words, by maintaining that our mortality, our annihilation, and our becoming-wholly-other in God, are all effectively thinkable. But how are these states conceivable as possibilities? On account of the fact that we are able to think – by dint of the absence of any reason for our being – a capacity-to-be-other capable of abolishing us, or of radically transforming us. But if so, then *this capacity-to-be-other cannot be conceived as a correlate of our thinking, precisely because it harbours the possibility of our own non-being.* In order to think myself as mortal, as the atheist does – and hence as capable of not being – I must think my capacity-not-to-be as an absolute possibility, for if I think this possibility as a correlate of my thinking, if I maintain that the possibility of my not-being only exists as a correlate of my act of thinking the possibility of my not-being, then *I can no longer conceive the possibility of my not-being*, which is precisely the thesis defended by the idealist. For I think myself as mortal only if I think that my death has no need of my thought of death in order to be actual. If my ceasing to be depended upon my continuing to be so that I could keep thinking myself as not being, then I would continue to agonize indefinitely, without ever actually passing away. In other words, in order to refute subjective idealism, I must grant that my possible annihilation is thinkable as something that is not just the correlate of my thought of this annihilation. Thus, the correlationist's refutation of idealism proceeds by way of an absolutization (which is to say, a de-correlation) of the capacity-to-be-other presupposed in the thought of facticity – this latter is the absolute whose reality is thinkable as that of the in-itself as such in its indifference to thought; an indifference which confers upon it the power to destroy me.

Even so, the correlationist might still make the following objection: 'The speculative thesis is no more certain than those of the realists and the idealist. For it is impossible to *give a reason* in favour of the hypothesis of the real possibility of every envisageable post-mortem eventuality, rather than in favour of the necessity of one among those states proposed by the dogmatic hypotheses. Thus, both the speculative and the metaphysical theses are equally conceivable, and we cannot decide between them.' But our answer to this must be that, on the contrary, there is indeed a precise reason for the superiority of the speculative thesis, and it is the agnostic herself who has provided us with it, viz., the agnostic cannot de-absolutize the capacity-to-be-other without thereby absolutizing it once again. For her objection, in effect, relies once more upon the conceivability of a capacity-to-be-other which must be thought of as absolute, thereby leaving every eventuality *open*, rather than closing them in favour of one of them alone, as the dogmatists do. The correlationist does the opposite of what she says – she says that we can think that a metaphysical thesis, which narrows the realm of possibility, might be true, rather than the speculative thesis, which leaves this realm entirely open; but she can only say this by thinking an open possibility, wherein no eventuality has any more reason to be realized than any other. This open possibility, this 'everything is equally possible', is an absolute that cannot be de-absolutized without being thought as absolute once more.

This is a point worth labouring, for the entirety of the preceding demonstration depends upon it. What the correlationist tells us is this: 'When I say that the metaphysical theses about the in-itself – call them M1 and M2 – are equally possible, the term "possible" here designates a *possibility of ignorance*. What I mean by this expression is that this possibility is merely a function of the fact that I do not know which is the correct thesis, M1 or M2. But I do not mean to claim that M1 or M2 are not necessary in-themselves, since the necessity of one of these eventualities could be real, but unfathomable. The speculative thesis is a third thesis which consists in maintaining that M1 and M2 are both *real possibilities*, either one of which is equally capable of being realized, perhaps even one after the other. But I maintain that we do not know which of these three theses – i.e. 1) necessity of M1; 2) necessity of M2; 3) real possibility of M1 and M2 – is true. Consequently, my claim is that what we are dealing with here is three possibilities of ignorance (1, 2, 3), and not with *two real possibilities* (M1, M2).'

Here now is the speculative philosopher's response: 'When you think of all three of these theses as "possible", how are you able to access this possibility? How are you able to *think* this "possibility of ignorance", which leaves all three eventualities open? The truth is that you are only able to think this possibility of ignorance because you have *actually* thought the *absoluteness* of this possibility, which is to say, its non-correlational character. Let me make myself clear, for this is the crux of the matter. So long as you maintain that your scepticism towards all knowledge of the absolute is based upon an argument, rather than upon mere belief or opinion, then you have to grant that the core of any such argument must be *thinkable*. But the core of your argument is that we *can* access everything's capacity-not-to-be, or capacity-to-be-other; our own as well as the world's. But once again, to say that one can think this is to say that one *can* think the absoluteness of the possibility of every thing. This is the price of distinguishing between the "in-itself" and the "for-us", since this difference is based upon the conceivability of the absolute's capacity-to-be-other relative to the given. Your general instrument of de-absolutization only works by conceding that what the speculative philosopher considers to be absolute is *actually thinkable* as an absolute; or better still, is actually *thought* – by you – as absolute, since were this not the case, *it would never have occurred to you not to be a subjective (or speculative) idealist.* The very idea of the difference between the in-itself and the for-us would never have arisen within you, had you not experienced what is perhaps human thought's most remarkable power – its capacity to access the possibility of its own non-being, and thus *to know* itself to be mortal. What you experience in your thought draws its redoubtable power from the profound truth which is implicated within it – you have "touched upon" nothing less than an absolute, the only veritable one, and with its help you have destroyed all the false absolutes of metaphysics, those of idealism as well as those of realism.

'Consequently, you are perfectly well able to distinguish between the possibility of ignorance and the possibility of the absolute. But this distinction will always be based upon the same argument – it is because one can think that it is absolutely possible for the in-itself to be other than the given, that what I believe to be really possible may not be really possible. Once this has been conceded, you are caught in an infinite regress, for every time you claim that what I call a real possibility is merely a possibility of ignorance, you will do so by way of an argument that works – i.e. continues to disqualify idealism, which is your other principal adversary – only by thinking as an absolute the possibility you claim to be de-absolutizing. In other words, one cannot think unreason – which is the equal and indifferent possibility of every eventuality – as merely relative to thought, since only by thinking it as an absolute can one de-absolutize every dogmatic thesis.'

We have now identified the faultline that lies right at the heart of correlationism; the one through which we can breach its defences – it is the fact that the argument of de-absolutization, which seemed unanswerable, can only function by carrying out an implicit absolutization of one of its two decisions. Either I choose – against idealism – to de-absolutize the correlation; but at the cost of absolutizing facticity. Or I choose, against the speculative philosopher, to de-absolutize facticity – I submit the latter to the primacy of the correlation (everything I think must be correlated with an act of thought) by asserting that this facticity is only true for-me, not necessarily in-itself. But this is at the cost of an idealist absolutization of the correlation – for my capacity-not-to-be becomes unthinkable once it is construed as nothing more than the correlate of my act of thought. Thus, correlationism cannot de-absolutize both of its principles at once, since it always needs one of them in order to de-absolutize the other. As a result, we have two ways out of the correlationist circle: either by absolutizing the correlation, or by absolutizing facticity. But we have already disqualified the metaphysical option by recusing the ontological argument; consequently, we cannot take the idealist path, which is still beholden to the idea of real necessity, according to which some deter-minate entity (Spirit, Will, Life), must absolutely be. It remains for us to follow the path of facticity, while taking care to ensure that its absoluti-zation not lead back to a dogmatic thesis.

***

It seems we have reached our goal, which was to identify the faultline in the correlationist circle that would allow us to cut through it towards an absolute. We must now try to clarify the meaning of this absolutization of facticity. We said that the absolute we seek should not be a dogmatic absolute: the illegitimacy of the ontological argument convinced us that all metaphysics – including the subjectivist metaphysics that eternalized the correlation – had to be refused, and with it every proposition of the type: this entity, or this determinate kind of entity, must absolutely be. Our task was to uncover an absolute that would not be an absolute entity. This is precisely what we obtain by absolutizing facticity – we do not maintain that a determinate entity exists, but that it is absolutely necessary that every entity might not exist. This is indeed a speculative thesis, since we are thinking an absolute, but it is not metaphysical, since we are not thinking any *thing* any (entity) that would *be* absolute. The absolute is the absolute impossibility of a necessary being. We are no longer upholding a variant of the principle of sufficient reason, according to which there is a necessary reason why everything is the way it is rather than otherwise, but rather the absolute truth of a *principle of unreason*. There is no reason for anything to be or to remain the way it is; everything must, without reason, be able not to be and/or be able to be other than it is.

What we have here is a *principle*, and even, we could say, an *anhypo-thetical* principle; not in the sense in which Plato used this term to describe the Idea of the Good, but rather in the Aristotelian sense. By 'anhypothetical principle', Aristotle meant a fundamental proposition that could not be deduced from any other, but which could be proved by argument.[1] This proof, which could be called 'indirect' or 'refutational', proceeds not by deducing the principle from some other proposition – in which we case it would no longer count as a principle – but by pointing out the inevitable inconsistency into which anyone contesting the truth of the principle is bound to fall. One establishes the principle without deducing it, by demonstrating that anyone who contests it can do so only by presupposing it to be true, thereby refuting him or herself. Aristotle sees in non-contradiction precisely such a principle, one that is established 'refutationally' rather than deductively, because any coherent challenge to it already presupposes its acceptance.[2] Yet there is an essential difference between the principle of unreason and the principle of non-contradiction; viz. what Aristotle demonstrates 'refutationally' is that no one can *think* a contradiction, but he has not thereby demonstrated that contradiction is absolutely impossible. Thus the strong correlationist could contrast the facticity of this principle to its absolutization – she would acknowledge that she cannot think contradiction, but she would refuse to acknowledge that this proves its absolute impossibility. For she will insist that nothing proves that what is possible in-itself might not differ *toto caelo* from what is thinkable for us. Consequently, the principle of non-contradiction is anhypothetical with regard to what is thinkable, but not with regard to what is possible.

By way of contrast, the principle of unreason is a principle that reveals itself to be not only *anhypothetical*, but also *absolute* – for as we have seen, one cannot contest its absolute validity without thereby presupposing its absolute truth. The sceptic is only able to conceive of the difference between the 'in-itself' and the 'for-us' by submitting the 'for-us' to an absence of reason which presupposes the absoluteness of the latter. It is because we can conceive of the absolute possibility that the 'in-itself' could be other than the 'for-us' that the correlationist argument can have any efficacy. Accordingly, the anhypotheticity of the principle of unreason pertains to the 'in-itself' as well as to the 'for-us', and thus to contest this principle is already to have presupposed it. Similarly, to query its absoluteness is already to have presupposed the latter.

This point becomes readily understandable if we relate this capacity-to-be-other-without-reason to the idea of a *time* that would be capable of bringing forth or abolishing everything. This is a time that cannot be conceived as having emerged or as being abolished except in time, which is to say, in itself. No doubt, this is a banal argument on the face of it: 'it is impossible to think the disappearance of time unless this disappearance occurs in time; consequently, the latter must be conceived to be eternal.' But what people fail to notice is that this banal argument can only work by presupposing a time that is not banal – not just a time whose capacity for destroying everything is a function of laws, but a time which is capable of the *lawless destruction of every physical law*. It is perfectly possible to conceive of a time determined by the governance of fixed laws disappearing in something other than itself – it would disappear in another time governed by *alternative* laws. But only the time that harbours the capacity to destroy every determinate reality, while obeying no determinate law – the time capable of destroying, without reason or law, both worlds and things – can be thought as an absolute. Only unreason can be thought as eternal, because only unreason can be thought as at once anhypothetical *and* absolute. Accordingly, we can say that it is possible to *demonstrate the absolute necessity of everything's non-necessity*. In other words, it is possible to establish, through indirect demonstration, the absolute necessity of the contingency of everything.

Yet this 'contingency' must be distinguished from the concept of the same name invoked earlier when we spoke of the empirical contingency of material objects. Facticity can be legitimately identified with contingency insofar as the former must not be thought of as comprising a possibility of ignorance, but rather as comprising a *positive knowledge* of everything's capacity-to-be-other or capacity-not-to-be. But absolute contingency differs from empirical contingency in the following way: empirical contingency – which we will henceforth refer to using the term 'precariousness' – generally designates a perishability that is bound to be realized sooner or later. This book, this fruit, this man, this star, are all bound to perish sooner or later, so long as physical and organic laws remain as they have been up until now. Thus 'precariousness' designates a possibility of not-being which must eventually be realized. By way of contrast, absolute contingency – for which we shall henceforth reserve the term 'contingency' – designates a *pure possibility*; one which may never be realized. For we cannot claim to know for sure whether or not our world, although it is contingent, will actually come to an end one day. We know, in accordance with the principle of unreason, that this is a real possibility, and that it could occur for no reason whatsoever; but we also know that there is nothing that necessitates it. To assert the opposite, viz., that everything must necessarily perish, would be to assert a proposition that is *still* metaphysical. Granted, this thesis of the precariousness of everything would no longer claim that a determinate entity is necessary, but it would continue to maintain that a determinate situation is necessary, viz., the destruction of this or that. But this is still to obey the injunction of the principle of reason, according to which there is a necessary reason why this is the case (the eventual destruction of X), rather than otherwise (the endless persistence of X). But we do not see by virtue of what there would be a reason necessitating the possibility of destruction as opposed to the possibility of persistence. The unequivocal relinquishment of the principle of reason requires us to insist that both the destruction and the perpetual preservation of a determinate entity must equally be able to occur for no reason. Contingency is such that anything might happen, even nothing at all, so that what is, remains as it is.

It now becomes possible to envisage a speculative critique of correlationism, for it becomes possible to demonstrate that the latter remains complicit with the fideist belief in the wholly-other insofar as it actually *continues* to remain faithful to the principle of reason. If the strong model of correlationism legitimates religious discourse in general, this is because it has failed to de-legitimate the possibility that there might be a hidden reason, an unfathomable purpose underlying the origin of our world. This reason has become unthinkable, but it has been preserved *as* unthinkable; sufficiently so to justify the value of its eventual unveiling in a transcendent revelation. This belief in an ultimate Reason reveals the true nature of strong correlationism – far from relinquishing the principle of reason, strong correlationism is in fact the apologia for the now irrational belief in this very principle. By way of contrast, speculation proceeds by *accentuating* thought's relinquishment of the principle of reason to the point where this relinquishment is converted into a principle, which alone allows us to grasp the fact that there is absolutely *no* ultimate Reason, whether thinkable or unthinkable. There is nothing beneath or beyond the manifest gratuitousness of the given – nothing but the limitless and lawless power of its destruction, emergence, or persistence.

***

We can now claim to have passed through the correlationist circle – or at least to have broken through the wall erected by the latter, which separated thought from the great outdoors, the eternal in-itself, whose being is indifferent to whether or not it is thought. We now know the location of the narrow passage through which thought is able to exit from itself – it is through facticity, and through facticity alone, that we are able to make our way towards the absolute.

Yet even were one to grant that we have indeed broken the circle, it would seem that this victory over correlationism has been won at such a cost, and with so many concessions to the latter, that ours is actually a Pyrrhic victory. For the only absolute we have managed to rescue from the confrontation would seem to be the very opposite of what is usually understood by that term, which is supposed to provide a foundation for knowledge. Our absolute, in effect, is nothing other than an extreme form of chaos, a *hyper-Chaos*, for which nothing is or would seem to be, impossible, not even the unthinkable. This absolute lies at the furthest remove from the absolutization we sought: the one that would allow mathematical science to describe the in-itself. We claimed that our absolutization of mathematics would conform to the Cartesian model and would proceed by identifying a primary absolute (the analogue of God), from which we would derive a secondary absolute, which is to say, a mathematical absolute (the analogue of extended substance). We have succeeded in identifying a primary absolute (Chaos), but contrary to the veracious God, the former would seem to be incapable of guaranteeing the absoluteness of scientific discourse, since, far from guaranteeing order, it guarantees only the possible destruction of every order.

If we look through the aperture which we have opened up onto the absolute, what we see there is a rather menacing power – something insensible, and capable of destroying both things and worlds, of bringing forth monstrous absurdities, yet also of never doing anything, of realizing every dream, but also every nightmare, of engendering random and frenetic transformations, or conversely, of producing a universe that remains motionless down to its ultimate recesses, like a cloud bearing the fiercest storms, then the eeriest bright spells, if only for an interval of disquieting calm. We see an omnipotence equal to that of the Cartesian God, and capable of anything, even the inconceivable; but an omnipotence that has become autonomous, without norms, blind, devoid of the other divine perfections, a power with neither goodness nor wisdom, ill-disposed to reassure thought about the veracity of its distinct ideas. We see something akin to Time, but a Time that is inconceivable for physics, since it is capable of destroying, without cause or reason, every physical law, just as it is inconceivable for metaphysics, since it is capable of destroying every determinate entity, even a god, even God. This is not a Heraclitean time, since it is not the eternal law of becoming, but rather the eternal and lawless possible becoming of every law. It is a Time capable of destroying even becoming itself by bringing forth, perhaps forever, fixity, stasis, and death.

How could such a disaster provide the foundation for scientific discourse? How could Chaos possibly legitimate knowledge of the ancestral?

In order to tackle this problem of the movement from our primary (chaotic) absolute, to our derived (mathematical) absolute, we must take a closer look at the transformation which we have wrought in the notion of facticity, by discovering in the latter a principle, rather than an ignorance of principle. So long as the proposition 'everything is possible, even the unthinkable' remained a correlationist proposition, we were dealing with a possibility of ignorance. What the sceptic meant by this proposition was that any thesis about the in-itself could, by right, be true, without anyone being able to discover which. And it seems that by maintaining the absoluteness of chaos we have gained nothing in terms of knowledge of the in-itself relative to the position of the sceptic – for instead of saying that the in-itself could actually be anything whatsoever without anyone knowing what, we maintain that the in-itself could actually be anything whatsoever and that we know this. What the sceptic construed as ignorance – everything is possible – we now construe as knowledge, but a knowledge whose content seems as indeterminate as the most complete ignorance.

Yet if we look more closely, we can detect a specific and significant difference between these two statements. If the correlationist's statement amounts to a pure avowal of ignorance, this is because she is incapable of disqualifying *any* hypothesis about the nature of the absolute – her claim is that it could be anything at all. But this is no longer the case when we construe facticity as an absolute. For we know two things that the sceptic did not: first, that contingency is necessary, and hence eternal; second, that contingency alone is necessary. But from this absolute necessity of contingency alone we can infer an impossibility that is every bit as absolute – for there is in fact something that this primary atom of knowledge ensures us is absolutely impossible, *even* for all powerful chaos, and this something, which chaos will never be able to produce, *is a necessary entity*. Everything is possible, anything can happen – except something that is necessary, because it is the contingency of the entity that is necessary, not the entity. Here we have a decisive difference between the principle of unreason and correlational facticity, for we now know that a metaphysical statement can *never* be true. We could certainly envisage the emergence of an entity which, *as a matter of fact*, would be indiscernible from a necessary entity, viz., an everlasting entity, which would go on existing, just like a necessary entity. Yet this entity would not be necessary, and we would not be able to say of it that it will actually last forever, only that, as a matter of fact, and up until now, it has never ceased to be. So what theoretical advantage can we expect to gain from these propositions, viz., 'only non-necessity is necessary', and 'nothing can exist that cannot but exist'?

These propositions are crucial because they harbour the principle of an *auto-limitation* or *auto-normalization of the omnipotence of chaos*. We can only hope to develop an absolute knowledge – a knowledge of chaos which would not simply keep repeating that everything is possible – on condition that we produce necessary propositions about it besides that of its omnipotence. But this requires that we discover norms or laws to which chaos itself is subject. Yet there is nothing over and above the power of chaos that could constrain it to submit to a norm. If chaos is subject to constraints, then this can only be a constraint which comes from the nature of chaos itself, from its own omnipotence. Now, the only necessity proper to chaos is that it remain chaos, and hence that there be nothing capable of resisting it – that *what is* always remain contingent, and that *what is* never be necessary. However – and here we come to the crux of the matter – our conviction is that in order for an entity to be contingent and un-necessary in this way, *it cannot be anything whatsoever*. This is to say that in order to be contingent and un-necessary, the entity must conform to *certain determinate conditions*, which can then be construed as *so many absolute properties of what is*. We then begin to understand what the rational discourse about unreason – an unreason which is not irrational – would consist in: it would be a discourse that aims to establish the constraints to which the entity must submit in order to exercise its capacity-not-to-be and its capacity-to-be-other.

What are these conditions, and how are we to obtain them?

We distinguished between two models of correlationism, the weak or Kantian model, which maintained the conceivability of the in-itself, and the strong model, which contested even this conceivability. The chaos which we have described thus far amounts to the 'objectification' of the possibility commensurate with the *strong* model, insofar as we described the former as capable of bringing about the unthinkable, the illogical, and the self-contradictory. Could we not 'curb' the potency of this chaos, so as to turn the latter into an 'objectification' of the *weak* or Kantian model instead? Might it not be possible to establish that chaos, *in order to* remain chaos, *cannot* actually bring forth the unthinkable? More precisely, we are asking whether the necessity of contingency might not impose the absolute truth of the two statements which Kant had formulated about the in-itself, and which ensured its conceivability:

1. The thing-in-itself is non-contradictory;
2. There is a thing-in-itself.

We are now going to see that these two statements about the in-itself, which Kant simply assumed without attempting to provide any further justification for them, can be demonstrated to be absolutely true through the principle of unreason. Let us see how.

***

We have obtained two ontological statements about unreason:

1. A necessary entity is impossible;
2. The contingency of the entity is necessary.

Although both these statements say more or less the same thing, their separate formulations are going to allow us to infer from them the *truth* of both of Kant's statements about the in-itself.

1. Here is the first thesis: *a contradictory entity is absolutely impossible, because if an entity was contradictory, it would be necessary.* But a necessary entity is absolutely impossible; consequently, so too is contradiction.

Since there is every likelihood that the reader will dismiss such an argument as nonsensical, it is probably best that we begin by examining the principal reasons why she is liable to refuse such an inference. More precisely, we will begin by expounding the objections against the very idea of a demonstration concerning non-contradiction, before entering into the internal logic of the argument.

a) First, it will be objected that there is nothing to say about a contradictory entity, since the latter is nothing, and nothing can be asserted about what is nothing.

But this is already to assume precisely what needs to be demonstrated, for how do we know that a contradictory entity is nothing? No doubt, a real contradiction is inconceivable, but the whole problem is to know what allows us to infer an absolute impossibility from this inconceivability. Thus, the objection that nothing can be said about contradiction because the contradictory is nothing simply begs the question, since one is indeed thereby asserting something about the contradictory entity, viz., that it is absolutely nothing, yet one is doing so without justifying this assertion, unlike the argument which one is supposedly criticizing.

b) Second, it will be objected that this argument is necessarily circular, since non-contradiction is presupposed in all rational argumentation. Consequently, the very claim to demonstrate the truth of non-contradiction is contradictory, since one's reasoning already assumes what is supposed to be demonstrated.

This objection also misconstrues what we are seeking to establish. We are not contesting the fact that non-contradiction is the minimal norm for all argumentation. But this principle by itself cannot suffice to guarantee the absolute impossibility of contradiction, since it stipulates the norm of the thinkable, not of the possible. We saw this in the case of Aristotle's construal of non-contradiction – the latter managed to establish this principle's necessity for thought, but not for the in-itself. There is no doubting the fact that our reasoning conforms to this principle, but this does not make it circular, since it proceeds only from the inconceivability of contradiction (which we assume), in order to infer the latter's impossibility, which is a distinct thesis. Our reasoning would only be circular if we assumed at the start the *impossibility* of contradiction. But it is not the absolute impossibility of contradiction which allows the argument to function; it is the absolute impossibility of necessity, which has been independently established through the anhypothetical principle of unreason. It is *because* the entity cannot be necessary – and not because the entity must be logically consistent – that we infer the impossibility of contradiction.

c) Now comes the third objection, which claims that our reasoning is well and truly circular, because in order to work, it has to presuppose what it is supposed to demonstrate, viz., the absolute impossibility (and not just the inconceivability) of contradiction. For if one does not assume the absolute status of contradiction, why then only infer from contradiction the necessity, and not also the contingency, of the entity? It is because it seems contradictory to us to maintain that an entity could be at once necessary and contingent that we infer from its being contradictory a determinate proposition, i.e. its being necessary, rather than its being contradictory, i.e. its being contingent. But why should chaos, which is supposed to be capable of producing the unthinkable, not be capable of rendering true the proposition 'what is necessary is contingent'? To deny this possibility is already to have assumed what one claimed to be demonstrating, viz., the absolute status of non-contradiction.

This third objection is the most serious. In order to refute it, we must explain the internal logic of our argument.

It is customary to construe those thinkers who affirmed the sheer becoming of all things as thinkers who maintained the reality of contradiction. The notion of real contradiction is then interpreted in terms of the idea of a flux in which every thing ceaselessly becomes other than it is, and wherein being passes ceaselessly into non-being, and non-being into being. Yet it seems to us profoundly inaccurate to associate the thesis of real contradiction with the thesis of sovereign flux. We have already put forward our own account of the universal becoming of all things: the latter consists in a chaos so chaotic that even becoming may arise and perish within it. But the only thing that could never arise and perish in such a chaos, the only thing that would remain exempt from all becoming as well as from all modification, the utterly Immutable instance against which even the omnipotence of contingency would come to grief, would be a contradictory entity. And this for the precise reason that such an entity could never become other than it is *because there would be no alterity for it in which to become*.

Let us suppose that a contradictory entity existed – what could possibly happen to it? Could it lapse into non-being? But it *is* contradictory, so that even if it happened not to be, it would still continue to be even in not-being, since this would be in conformity with its paradoxical 'essence'. It would exemplify the truth of the proposition: 'what is, is not, and what is not, is.' Perhaps it might be objected that in such a case, one could neither say that it is or that it is not? But this is not an option, since we are already *assuming* that such a contradictory entity exists. Therefore, by hypothesis, this entity exists, and so we must be content simply to examine *the way in which* this contradictory entity can exist. But it then becomes apparent that one of the defining characteristics of such an entity would be to continue to be even were it not to be. Consequently, if this entity existed, it would be impossible for it simply to cease to exist – unperturbed, it would incorporate the fact of not existing into its being. Thus, as an instance of a *really* contradictory being, this entity would be *perfectly eternal*.

Yet this entity would also prove incapable of undergoing any sort of actual becoming – it could never become other than it is, since it already *is* this other. As contradictory, this entity is always-already whatever it is not. Thus, the introduction of a contradictory entity into being would result in the implosion of the very idea of determination – of being such and such, of being this rather than that. Such an entity would be tantamount to a 'black hole of differences', into which all alterity would be irremediably swallowed up, since the being-other of this entity would be obliged, simply by virtue of being other than it, *not* to be other than it. Accordingly, real contradiction can in no way be identified with the thesis of universal becoming, for in becoming, things must be this, *then* other than this; they are, *then* they are not. This does not involve *any* contradiction, since the entity is never simultaneously this and its opposite, existent and non-existent. A really illogical entity consists rather in the systematic destruction of the minimal conditions for all becoming – it suppresses the dimension of alterity required for the deployment of any process whatsoever, liquidating it in the formless being which must always already be what it is not. Thus it is not by chance that the greatest thinker of contradiction, that is to say, Hegel, was not the thinker of the sovereignty of becoming, but on the contrary, the thinker of absolute identity, of the identity of identity and difference. For what Hegel saw so acutely is that the necessary entity *par excellence* could only be the entity that had nothing outside it and that would not be limited by any alterity. Thus the Supreme Being could only be the being that remains in itself even as it passes into its other, the entity that contains contradiction within itself as a moment of its own development, the entity that verifies the supreme contradiction of not becoming anything other even as it becomes other. It is supreme, reposing eternally within itself, because it absorbs both difference and becoming into its superior identity. And it harbours the superior form of eternity because it is at once temporal and atemporal, processual and immutable.

We are now in a position to see why the third objection outlined above is invalid. This objection claimed that by inferring the necessity of the entity from its being-contradictory, we were already presupposing the absoluteness of the principle of non-contradiction, for otherwise we could just as well have inferred the entity's contingency. To this we must reply that *one may* certainly say of a contradictory entity that it is at once necessary and unnecessary, but in doing so, one continues to describe it as a supremely necessary entity, since one continues to preclude any dimension of alterity through which the entity could be subjected to change. Although one may *say* anything at all about a contradictory entity, nevertheless, one is thereby *doing* something very specific, because one is *indistinguishing* everything, and consequently eliminating any possibility of thinking this entity's being-otherwise. The only possibility of reintroducing difference into being, and thereby a conceivable becoming, would be by no longer allowing oneself the right to make contradictory statements about an entity.

Consequently, we know by the principle of unreason why non-contradiction is an absolute ontological truth: because it is necessary that what is be determined in such a way as to be *capable of becoming*, and of being subsequently determined in *some other* way. It is necessary that this be this and not that, or anything else whatsoever, precisely in order to ensure that this can become that or anything else whatsoever. Accordingly, it becomes apparent that the ontological meaning of the principle of non-contradiction, far from designating any sort of fixed essence, *is that of the necessity of contingency, or in other words, of the omnipotence of chaos*.

Leibniz founded metaphysical rationality upon two principles whose scope was considered to be absolute: the principle of non-contradiction and the principle of sufficient reason.[3] Hegel saw that the absolutization of the principle of sufficient reason (which marked the culmination of the belief in the necessity of what is) required the devaluation of the principle of non-contradiction. Strong (Wittgensteinian-Heideggerian) correlationism insisted upon de-absolutizing both the principle of reason and the principle of non-contradiction. But the principle of unreason teaches us that *it is because the principle of reason is absolutely false that the principle of non-contradiction is absolutely true*.

2. We move now to the second question. This time it is a matter of demonstrating the thesis which states that the thing-in-itself actually exists, and that there is a realm of the in-itself, and not just the phenomenal realm of the 'for-us'. We will call this the thesis of the 'there is'. Ultimately, this boils down to confronting the Leibnizian question: 'why is there something rather than nothing?' It is a matter of demonstrating that it is absolutely necessary that the in-itself exists, and hence that the latter cannot dissolve into nothingness, whereas on the contrary, the realm of the 'for-us' is essentially perishable, since it remains correlative with the existence of thinking and/or living beings. We must demonstrate that everything would not lapse into nothingness with the annihilation of living creatures, and that the world in-itself would subsist despite the abolition of every relation-to-the-world.

But we do not propose to formulate (or resolve) this question in the manner of metaphysicians, which is to say, by unveiling the existence of a Prime Mover or Supreme Being which would supposedly provide the reason for the fact that there is anything at all. What we propose to do is offer a resolution of this problem which would be at once non-theological (foregoing any appeal to an ultimate reason) and non-fideist. Our aim is to recuse both of these attitudes to the question – the metaphysical attitude, which resolves it by using the principle of reason and by invoking a Supreme Reason; and the fideist attitude, which maintains ironically that the question has no meaning for philosophy – not in order to abolish it, but only so as to hand it over to some non-rational discourse. Our suggestion here is that it is not the atheist but rather the believer – in his contemporary sceptico-fideist incarnation – who insists that Leibniz's question has no rational meaning. For in doing so, the believer is able to endow the question with a purely religious significance, whereby being is construed as the manifestation of a prodigy, a miraculous deliverance from nothingness – a miracle which, since it is gratuitous and un-necessary, can be construed as fragile and reversible. Ultimately, the fideist is someone who marvels at the fact that there is something rather than nothing because he believes that there is no reason for it, and that being is a pure gift, which might never have occurred.

Consequently, there are two positions which we have to counter: the one that claims to provide a rational answer to the question by invoking a God or Ultimate Principle, and the one that claims to deliver the question from the jurisdiction of reason to the benefit of God or some instance of the Wholly Other. In other words, we must criticize the dogmatic resolution of the question as well as its ironic dissolution, whose theoretical scepticism actually perpetuates (whether avowedly or not) its religious meaning, which alone is deemed capable of extolling its profundity.

Faced with these two ways of endowing the problem with an elevated meaning – a meaning which in both cases leads straight to the divine – the speculative stance requires that we treat the question prosaically. The point is to de-dramatize this question, to reduce it to its proper degree of importance, which is not zero, but secondary. Thus the question *must* be resolved, since claims that it is insoluble or meaningless are just another way of legitimating its continuing exaltation. But instead of elevating us to the eminence of a first cause, its resolution should serve rather as a reminder of the latter's eternal absence. We must free ourselves of the question – but this requires not just that we resolve it, but that we formulate an answer to it which is necessarily disappointing, so that this disappointment becomes its most instructive aspect. The only proper attitude when confronted with such a problem is to maintain that there is little at stake in it, and that the spiritual tremulousness which it inspires, whether sardonic or profound, is inappropriate. Among the speculative criteria for the proper solution to the problem should be the sobering effect induced in the reader when she understands the solution, and says to herself, 'so that's what it was …'

So let us attempt a deflationary solution.

Ultimately, this derivation of the 'there is' is a matter of specifying the meaning of the statement from which we began: facticity is absolute, it is not a fact which might not be the case. The meaning of the principle of unreason consists in the claim that facticity is not just another fact in the world – facticity is not on the same level as facts, like an extra fact which could be added to the latter. I can doubt the permanence of facts, but I cannot doubt the permanence of facticity without thereby reiterating it as an absolute. Yet this statement about the non-facticity of facticity can be understood in two ways, which we will refer to as the *weak* and *strong* interpretations of the principle of unreason.

The weak interpretation of the principle can be formulated as follows: to say that contingency is necessary is to say that *if* something is, then it must be contingent. The strong interpretation, by way of contrast, maintains the following: to say that contingency is necessary, is to say *both* that things must be contingent *and* that there must be contingent things. The weak interpretation claims that it is not just a fact – one more fact alongside others – that existing things are factual, as opposed to necessary; but the strong interpretation also claims that neither is it a fact – one more fact alongside others – that factual things exist, as opposed to not existing.

If one accepts the principle of unreason, one is at least committed to its weak interpretation – this is the minimal sense of the principle, according to which if something is, then it must be contingent. To reject the weak interpretation would be to reject the principle of unreason. But since, by hypothesis, we have already accepted the principle, then we must also accept its weak interpretation. But one could very well accept the principle of factuality while rejecting its strong interpretation – thus one could maintain that *if* something exists, then it must be contingent, while insisting that this in no way entails that something *must* exist – if things exist, then they necessarily exist as facts, but nothing necessitates that there be factual things. Consequently, the question 'why is there something rather than nothing?' takes the following form for us: can one, contrary to the preceding thesis which confines itself to the weak interpretation, *justify a strong interpretation of the principle of unreason*? If this interpretation were to be accepted, then we would have succeeded in establishing that it is necessary that something exist, because it is necessary that contingent things exist.

In order to try and legitimate the strong interpretation, let us begin by assuming that only the weak interpretation is valid. If so, what exactly would this entail? We would have to say that it is a fact, not a necessity, that factual things exist. Thus, the very existence of facticity would have to be described as a fact, for if nothing existed, then nothing would be factual, and consequently there would be no facticity. But the only way for me to maintain such a thesis would be by asserting a facticity of facticity, which is to say, a 'second-order' facticity. I would have to claim that there is a first-order facticity, which would be the facticity of things, and which entails that it is possible for every determinate structure or thing not to exist; but also a second-order facticity, a facticity of the facticity of things, which would entail that first-order facticity might not obtain in the absence of the *actual existence* of factual things. But if we recall how we established the principle of unreason, it is easy to see that this thesis is self-refuting. For as we saw earlier, in order to doubt the necessity of something, I must grant that the facticity of this thing can be thought as an absolute. Moreover, in order for the world in its entirety to be thought as capable of not being, or of not being as it is, I must assume that the possibility of its not-being (its facticity) can be thought by me as an absolute (and thus as not just the correlate of my thought). Or again, as we saw above, in order to grasp my own mortality, I must construe my death, the possibility of my not-being, as an absolute possibility. Accordingly, I cannot doubt the absoluteness of facticity without immediately re-instating it as an absolute. When I claim that the facticity of things (first-order facticity) is a fact, I also assume that the facticity of facticity (second-order facticity) can be thought as an absolute. But then I become caught in an infinite regress, for if I claim that second-order facticity is also a fact, I can only do so by assuming that there is a third-order facticity which is itself absolute, and so on.

In other words, the act of doubting the necessity of facticity is self-refuting, because it assumes an absoluteness of facticity in the *act* of thinking while simultaneously denying it in the content of this same thought. Accordingly, facticity cannot be thought of as another fact in the world – it is not a fact that things are factual, juts as it is not a fact that factual things exist. Thus the only coherent interpretation of the principle of factuality is the strong one: it is not a fact but rather an absolute necessity that factual things exist.

Yet here we can envisage another objection, which we will once more set forth in the form of a direct discourse: 'Your thesis is invalid for the following reason: contingency designates not only positive facts pertaining to existing things or events that could have not existed (such as, for example, the fact that "this leaf is on my table"), but also "negative facts" pertaining to non-existing things or events that could have existed but didn't (such as for example the fact that "it is not raining today"). Thus to say that contingency is necessary is to say that it is necessary that there be non-existing things that could exist (negative facts that have no reason to remain negative), as well as existing things that could not-exist. Why then not say that contingency could subsist as the contingency *of negative facts alone*? This would mean that there are non-existing things capable of existing, but there are no existing things capable of not-existing. Everything would remain "potential" in the midst of chaos without facticity being abolished, since a negative fact remains a fact. Contingency would pertain only to eventualities or propensities to be, none of which would have been actualized – it would be contingent that propensities remain mere propensities, yet in fact, none of them would have been actualized. For after all, if one is willing to admit that something that exists could, in fact, continue to exist indefinitely, then one must also admit that anything that does not exist could, in fact, continue to persist indefinitely in its virtual-being.'

This objection can be refuted as follows: although our interlocutor does not deny that facticity can be thought as an absolute, she maintains that this absoluteness can be thought as the (eventual) absoluteness of negative facts alone. Thus the necessity of facticity is no longer the guarantor of the existence of positive facts. Yet to admit that facticity can be thought as an absolute is *a fortiori* to admit that it can be thought full stop. But I cannot think facticity *merely* as the possibility that existing things could not exist, *or* that non-existing things could exist – the persistence of the two realms of existence and non-existence provides the very condition for the conceivability of facticity. For although I can think the contingency of this existing thing, I cannot think the contingency of *existence* as such (or of the fact that something exists in general). Thus, I am perfectly incapable of thinking the abolition of existence, and so becoming-inexistent is only conceivable as the becoming of a *determinate* existent, not as the becoming of existence in general. To claim that an existent can not exist, and to claim moreover that this possibility is an ontological necessity, is also to claim that the sheer existence of the existent, just like the sheer inexistence of the inexistent, are the two imperishable poles which allow the perishability of everything to be thought. Consequently, I can no more conceive of the contingency of negative facts alone than I can conceive of the non-being of existence as such. Since contingency is thinkable (as an absolute), but unthinkable without the persistence of the two realms of existence and inexistence, we have to say that it is necessary that there always be this or that existent capable of not existing, and this or that inexistent capable of existing.

Thus the solution to the problem is as follows: *it is necessary that there be something rather than nothing because it is necessarily contingent that there is something rather than something else.* The necessity of the contingency of the entity imposes the necessary existence of the contingent entity.

In the context of transcendental idealism, the unsurpassable facticity of the *a priori* forms of representation prohibited the identification of the latter with the properties of the thing-in-itself – this facticity precluded the speculative deduction of the categories as necessary properties of the in-itself. Thus, facticity constituted the core of Kant's Critical de-absoluti-zation. Yet Kant infringed the limits he had imposed upon our ability to think the in-itself on two counts, without making any serious attempt to justify this infringement – he assumed that the thing-in-itself existed, and he assumed that it was non-contradictory.

By way of contrast, non-metaphysical speculation proceeds in the first instance by stating that the thing-in-itself is nothing other than the facticity of the transcendental forms of representation. Then, in the second instance, it goes on to deduce from the absoluteness of this facticity those properties of the in-itself which Kant for his part took to be self-evident.

***

Philosophy is the invention of strange forms of argumentation, neces-sarily bordering on sophistry, which remains its dark structural double. To philosophize is always to develop an idea whose elaboration and defence require a novel kind of argumentation, the model for which lies neither in positive science – not even in logic – nor in some supposedly innate faculty for proper reasoning. Thus it is essential that a philosophy produce internal mechanisms for regulating its own inferences – signposts and criticisms through which the newly constituted domain is equipped with a set of constraints that provide internal criteria for distinguishing between licit and illicit claims.

Far from seeing in criticism a threat to its consistency, the examination of the determinate conditions for absolute unreason should strive to multiply objections, the better to reinforce the binding texture of its argumentative fabric. It is by exposing the weaknesses in our own arguments that we will uncover, by way of a meticulous, step by step examination of the inadequacies in our reasoning, the idea of a non-metaphysical and non-religious discourse on the absolute. For it is by progressively uncovering new problems, and adequate responses to them, that we will give life and existence to a *logos* of contingency, which is to say, a reason emancipated from the principle of reason – a *speculative form of the rational* that would no longer be a *metaphysical reason*.

Here is but one example of such a problematization of the speculative approach. We claimed to have established the necessity of non-contradiction because a contradictory being would be a necessary being. But it could be objected that we have conflated *contradiction* and *inconsistency*. In formal logic, an 'inconsistent system' is a formal system all of whose well-formed statements are true. If this formal system comprises the operator of negation, we say that an axiomatic is inconsistent if *every* contradiction which can be formulated within it is true. By way of contrast, a formal system is said to be non-contradictory when (being equipped with the operator of negation) it does not allow *any* contradiction to be true. Accordingly, it is perfectly possible for a logical system to *be* contradictory without thereby being inconsistent – all that is required is that it give rise to *some* contradictory statements which are true, without permitting *every* contradiction to be true. This is the case with 'paraconsistent' logics, in which some but not all contradictions are true.[4] Clearly then, for contemporary logicians, it is not non-contradiction that provides the criterion for what is thinkable, but rather inconsistency. What every logic – as well as every *logos* more generally – wants to avoid is a discourse so trivial that it renders every well-formulated statement, as well as its negation, equally valid. But contradiction is logically thinkable so long as it remains 'confined' within limits such that it does not entail the truth of every contradiction.

Consequently, our thesis is inadequate on two counts:

1. We maintained that contradiction is unthinkable, whereas it is logically conceivable.

2. We claimed that a contradictory being would be indistinguishable from every other being, whereas in fact this would only be the case for an inconsistent being. For only with regard to an inconsistent being could one maintain every proposition as well as its negation. Yet it is possible to conceive of a world wherein *one* particular contradiction would be true (e.g. a mare that is not a mare), but not *another* contradiction (e.g. a featherless biped that is not a biped). Accordingly, it becomes possible to think a plurality of contradictory worlds, each different from the other. These worlds could be considered to be contingent in conformity with the speculative criteria outlined above, since it would be perfectly conceivable for them to become other than they are now – thus, a world embodying contradiction A could *become* a world no longer embodying contradiction A but contradiction B, or both A and B, etc. But if a contradictory being can be thought as contingent, then we have not refuted its possibility in light of the principle of unreason. Such considerations might also lead one to conclude that we have not convincingly refuted the Hegelian dialectic, since the latter never maintains the being-true of every contradiction, but only of certain determinate contradictions that give rise to other determinate contradictions – thus, the dialectic is contradictory, but not inconsistent.

Yet far from undermining our speculative enquiry, this objection from paraconsistent logic provides us with an opportunity to flesh it out. We would need to do this in two steps:

1. In the first step, we would need to correct our thesis by reformulating it in terms of consistency – what we have actually demonstrated is that an inconsistent being is impossible because it would be necessary if it existed. Thus, our first task would be to verify that the reasoning through which we arrived at the impossibility of contradiction also manages to establish the claim 'nothing can be *inconsistent* because nothing can *be* necessary'.

2. In the second step, the speculative enquiry would need to be extended so as to include contradiction itself. This time the question would be to know whether or not we could also use the principle of unreason to disqualify the possibility of *real* contradiction. We would need to point out that paraconsistent logics were not developed in order to account for actual contradictory facts, but only in order to prevent

computers, such as expert medical systems, from deducing anything whatsoever from contradictory *data* (for instance, conflicting diagnoses about a single case), because of the principle of *ex falso quodlibet*.[5] Thus, it would be a matter of ascertaining whether contradiction, which can be conceived in terms of incoherent data about the world, can still be conceived in terms of non-linguistic occurrences. We would then have to try to demonstrate that dialectics and paraconsistent logics are only ever dealing with contradictions inherent in *statements* about the world, never with *real* contradictions in the world – in other words, they deal with contradictory theses about a single reality, rather than with a contradictory reality. Dialectics and paraconsistent logics would be shown to be studies of the ways in which the contradictions of thought produce effects in thought, rather than studies of the supposedly ontological contradictions which thought discovers in the surrounding world. Finally, our investigation would have to conclude by demonstrating that real contradiction and real inconsistency both violate the conditions for the conceivability of contingency.

We will not pursue this investigation any further here – we merely wished to suggest that, far from culminating in irrationality, the principle of unreason allows us to generate a domain of specific problems wherein the *logos* may progressively unfold the axes of its argumentation.

***

Let us settle on a terminology. From now on, we will use the term 'factiality' [*factualité*][6] to describe the speculative essence of *facticity*, viz., that the facticity of every thing cannot be thought as a fact. Thus factiality must be understood as the non-facticity of facticity. We will call 'non-iterability of facticity' the impossibility of applying facticity to itself – this non-iterability describes the genesis of the only absolute necessity available to non-dogmatic speculation – the necessity for everything that is to be a fact. Accordingly, from now on, we will replace the expression 'principle of unreason', which has the inconvenience of being purely negative, with the expression 'principle of factiality', which provides a positive determination of the actual domain of our investigation, viz., that of the non-factual essence of fact as such, which is to say, its necessity, as well as that of its determinate conditions. To be is necessarily to be a fact, but to be a fact is not just to be anything whatsoever. We will call 'factial' [*factuale*] the type of speculation which seeks and identifies the conditions of factiality (but we will sometimes say 'the factial' for short when speaking of this speculative register). We will call 'derivation' the demonstration which establishes that a statement is a condition of facticity. Lastly, we will refer to these conditions, which include non-contradiction and the 'there is' (i.e. that there is something rather than nothing), as 'figures'.

Accordingly, the principle of factiality can be stated as follows: *only facticity is not factual* – viz., only the contingency of what is, is not itself contingent. But it is important to bear in mind the following: the principle of factiality does *not* claim that contingency is necessary; its precise claim is that contingency *alone* is necessary – and only this prevents it from being metaphysical. For the statement 'contingency is necessary' is in fact entirely compatible with metaphysics. Thus, Hegelian metaphysics maintains the necessity of a moment of irremediable contingency in the unfolding of the absolute; a moment that occurs in the midst of nature as the pure contingency, the reality devoid of actuality, the sheer finitude whose chaos and gratuitousness are recalcitrant to the labour of the Notion, but through which the infinite – to which nothing can remain external, for this would limit it and render it finite – must pass. Accordingly, for Hegel, the fact that nature only partially corresponds to the Hegelian concept of nature is the mark of the former's necessary defectiveness – a defectiveness through which the absolute must pass in order to be absolute. For it is necessary that there be a moment of sheer irrationality in the midst of the unfolding of the absolute – a contingency that is peripheral yet real, providing the Whole with a guarantee that the irrational does not subsist outside it, and thereby ensuring that the latter truly is the Whole.[7] But this contingency is deduced from the unfolding of the absolute, which in itself, *qua* rational totality, is devoid of contingency. Thus, in Hegel, the necessity of contingency is not derived from contingency as such and contingency alone, but from a Whole that is ontologically superior to the latter. This is precisely what separates the factial from the dialectical – or to put it more generally, and using our own terminology, what separates the speculative from the metaphysical.[7]

By formulating a speculative principle and identifying a specific procedure of derivation, we have managed to put in place what we set out to look for, viz., the possibility of resolving the problem of ancestrality by absolutizing mathematical discourse. Consequently, the problem can now be stated as follows: we have derived from the principle of factiality two propositions – non-contradiction and the necessity of the 'there is' – which have allowed us to secure Kant's thesis about the conceivability of the thing-in-itself. In our determination of chaos, we moved from the thesis of strong correlationism (chaos can do anything whatsoever), to the thesis of weak correlationism (chaos can do anything except for the unthinkable). Thus, for the moment, we 'occupy' a Kantian in-itself. Consequently, in order to legitimate science's ancestral discourse, we must now realize, by way of a factial derivation, *the transition from the truth of the Kantian in-itself to the truth of the Cartesian in-itself* – a transition wherein it is no longer the *logical* principle of non-contradiction that is absolutized, but rather the *mathematical* statement *qua* mathematical.

As we said earlier, we cannot present the complete resolution of the problem here. So we shall content ourselves with providing a more precise formulation of the question of ancestrality by further specifying what we mean by 'mathematical' and what we mean to absolutize through this vocable.

Chapter 4
Hume's Problem

So long as we believe that there must be a reason why what is, is the way it is, we will continue to fuel superstition, which is to say, the belief that there is an ineffable reason underlying all things. Since we will never be able to discover or understand such a reason, all we can do is believe in it, or aspire to believe in it. So long as we construe our access to facticity in terms of thought's discovery of its own intrinsic limits and of its inability to uncover the ultimate reason for things, our abolition of metaphysics will only have served to resuscitate religiosity in all its forms, including the most menacing ones. So long as we construe facticity as a limit for thought, we will abandon whatever lies beyond this limit to the rule of piety. Thus, in order to interrupt this see-sawing between metaphysics and fideism, we must transform our perspective on unreason, stop construing it as the form of our deficient grasp of the world and turn it into the veridical content of this world as such – we must project unreason into things themselves, and discover in our grasp of facticity the veritable *intellectual intuition* of the absolute. 'Intuition', because it is actually in what is that we discover a contingency with no limit other than itself; 'intellectual' because this contingency is neither visible nor perceptible in things and only thought is capable of accessing it, just as it accesses the chaos that underlies the apparent continuity of phenomena.

No doubt, this is yet another bid to overturn Platonism, but it differs fundamentally from those with which we are all familiar. Unlike Nietzsche, it is not a matter of abolishing the immutable realm of ideality on behalf of the sensible becoming of all things, nor even of relinquishing traditional philosophical denunciations of phenomenal time and of the illusions of the senses. Rather, it is a matter of relinquishing the belief, common to Platonism and anti-Platonism, that becoming pertains to phenomena while intelligibility pertains to the immutable, and of denouncing, via intellectual intuition, the *'stabilist' illusion of sensible becoming* – the illusion that there are invariants or immutable laws of becoming. The speculative releases us from the phenomenal stability of empirical constants by elevating us to the purely intelligible chaos that underlies every aspect of it.

We said above that so long as we continue to believe that there is a reason why things are the way they are rather than some other way, we will construe this world as a mystery, since no such reason will ever be vouchsafed to us. And yet – we come now to the issue that is going to occupy us – the requirement that there be a necessitating reason is not just a symptom of ideological delusion or of theoretical timorousness. It follows from a principled rejection of the factial based upon an apparently decisive objection against the latter; an objection which we shall have to expound and refute if we want our speculative approach to retain a minimal degree of credibility.

This objection is the following: it seems absurd to maintain that not only things but also physical laws are really contingent, for if this was the case, we would have to admit that these laws could actually *change at any moment for no reason whatsoever.*

And indeed, one unavoidable consequence of the principle of factiality is that it asserts the actual contingency of the laws of nature. If we are seriously maintaining that everything that *seems* to us to have no reason to be the way it is, *is* actually devoid of any necessary reason to be the way it is, and could actually change for no reason, then we must seriously maintain that the laws of nature could change, not in accordance with some superior hidden law – the law of the modification of laws, which we could once more construe as the mysterious and immutable constant governing all subordinate transformations – but for no cause or reason whatsoever.

However, the objection continues, anyone who accepts the foregoing thesis would have to expect objects to behave in the most capricious fashion at every moment, and thank the heavens that this is not the case, and that things continue to conform to everyday constants. Those of us who endorse this claim would have to spend our time fearing that familiar objects could at any moment behave in the most unexpected ways, congratulating ourselves every evening on having made it through the day without a hitch – before worrying about what the night might hold in store. Such a conception of reality or relation-to-the-world seems so absurd that no one could sincerely maintain it. We all know the old adage according to which there is no absurdity that has not at one time or another been seriously defended by some philosopher. Our objector might acerbically remark that we have just proved this adage false, for there was one absurdity that no one had yet proclaimed, and we have just unearthed it.

Our objector will conclude that we have no choice but to admit that laws are underwritten by a necessity that rules out such capricious disorder. Since this real necessity cannot be derived from logic or mathematics alone – for we can conceive of many physical universes other than our own without contradiction – there is nothing for it but to maintain that the world is underwritten by a necessity that is not logico-mathematical but rather intrinsically physical, and for which it will always be impossible to provide a comprehensible reason. But – and here is the crux of the objection – we cannot give up the idea of such a necessity on the grounds of its enigmatic character *without also giving up the manifest stability of our world*. For, short of stupefying coincidence, a world without physical necessity would be riven at each instant and in each of its points by an immense multiplicity of disconnected possibilities, on account of which it would implode into a radical disorder infusing even its tiniest material particles. In other words, the objection goes, if physical laws were actually contingent, *we would already have noticed it* – moreover, it is quite likely that we would not even be here to notice it, since the disorder resulting from such contingency would no doubt have atomized all consciousness, as well as the world that is given to it to perceive. Thus, the *fact* of the *stability* of the laws of nature seems sufficient to refute the very idea of their possible contingency – unless, of course, we were to attribute this stability to a quite extraordinary degree of coincidence, which would have allowed us to live up until now amidst constants of quite impeccable stability – a statistical miracle which we would have good reason to marvel at, but whose imminent collapse, whether in the coming day or the coming minute, we would also have every reason to fear.

But it is precisely this claim about the real contingency of physical laws that we propose to defend in all seriousness. Yet we do not give thanks at every instant that we live in a stable world. For although we maintain that the laws of nature could actually change for no reason, nevertheless, like everyone else, we do not expect them to change *incessantly*. In other words, our claim is that it is possible to sincerely maintain that objects could *actually and for no reason whatsoever* behave in the most erratic fashion, without having to modify our usual everyday relation to things. This is what we must now attempt to justify.

***

The difficulty which we have just identified is a familiar philosophical problem – it is known as 'Hume's problem'. To answer the foregoing criticism of the claim that physical laws are contingent is *to propose a speculative solution to Hume's problem.*

What is this problem? In its traditional version, it can be formulated as follows: is it possible to demonstrate that the same effects will always follow from the same causes *ceteris paribus*, i.e. all other things being equal? In other words, can one establish that in identical circumstances, future successions of phenomena will always be identical to previous successions? The question raised by Hume concerns our capacity to demonstrate the necessity of the causal connection.[1]

Our account will focus on the principle of causality, also known as 'the principle of the uniformity of nature' by those suspicious of the term 'cause'. Whatever name one prefers, the formulation is essentially the same: this principle assumes that given the same initial conditions, the same results invariably follow. However, we must dispel an all too frequent misunderstanding here by pointing out that the necessity of this principle has never been seriously called into question by the varieties of falsificationism inaugurated by Karl Popper. Falsificationism does not claim that the laws of nature could change for no reason in the future, but 'only' that the *theories* espoused by the sciences of nature are always susceptible to refutation by *unexpected* experimental results. For falsificationism, it is a matter of being forced to reconsider our belief in the permanence of physical theories because of the impossibility of attaining certain knowledge of the 'active factors' that may be present in nature. Thus neither Popper nor any other epistemologist claims that a theory could be subverted because of a *random* transformation in the structure of reality. Popper does not maintain that given *identical* circumstances, physical laws could some day change – he maintains only that we can never demonstrate that a determinate physical theory will always be valid, since it is impossible to rule out *a priori* the future possibility of an experiment behaving in the manner of an *as yet un-catalogued* datum that could invalidate the predictions of the theory in question. Physicists were driven to abandon Newtonian physics in favour of Relativity physics by new experiments, or new interpretations of old experiments, not by some sudden transformation in the structure of nature occurring sometime around 1905 (the date of the publication of the Special Theory of Relativity), and which modified the physical universe itself. Thus Popper assumes without further argument that the principle of the uniformity of nature is veridical, and never genuinely confronts Hume's problem, which is not about the question of the future validity of our theories of nature, but about the future stability of nature itself.[2]

We must also make a further clarification. The problem of causality as raised by Hume is a problem that concerns the constancy of natural laws regardless of whether these are construed *deterministically* or *indeterministically*, i.e. probabilistically. Obviously, Hume formulated his problem within the deterministic framework of the physics of his day, but the nature of the problem is actually unaffected by the question of whether or not natural laws will turn out to be probabilistic. It is a matter of knowing whether given perfectly identical circumstances, the same laws will be verified in the future, irrespective of the nature of these laws. In the case of a deterministic law, we would have to ask whether given conditions X then event Y, and only event Y, will continue to occur tomorrow in the same way it occurred today. In the case of a probabilistic law, we would have to ask whether given conditions X, event Y will have the same probability of occurring or not occurring tomorrow as it does today. Thus, the problem of causality as formulated by Hume must not be conflated with the problem of determinism – it is a more general problem concerning all laws of nature, irrespective of their eventual specificity.

The same point can be put differently by saying that Hume's problem raises the question of whether we can have any guarantee that physics *as such* – and not just this or that variety of physics – will continue to be possible in the future. The condition of possibility for physics is the repeatability of experiments, which is the fundamental guarantor of the validity of a theory. But if we found tomorrow that successive experiments carried out under exactly the same conditions yielded completely different results, if it became impossible to guarantee stable effects or stable probabilities from one day to the next for the same experimental conditions, then it is the very idea of physical science that would be undermined. Thus, Hume's question can be formulated as follows: can we demonstrate that the experimental science which is possible today will still be possible tomorrow?

This is the proper formulation of the problem, to which up until now, three types of responses have been envisaged: a *metaphysical* response, a *sceptical* response (the one espoused by Hume himself), and of course Kant's *transcendental* response. We will briefly reiterate the essential elements of all three responses before outlining those of the *speculative* response.

1. A metaphysical response to Hume's question would proceed by demonstrating the existence of a supreme principle governing our world. Thus, for instance, one might proceed in the manner of a disciple of Leibniz, and begin by demonstrating the necessary existence of a perfect God, before proceeding to infer from the latter fact that such a God can only have created the best of all possible worlds, which is to say, ours. Accordingly, the eternity of our world, or at least of the principles that govern it, would be guaranteed by the eternity of divine perfection itself. This would be what could be called a *direct* and *unconditional* proof of causal necessity – I produce a positive demonstration that the existence of God is unconditionally necessary (that it proceeds from His essence alone, rather than from some external condition), before directly inferring from it that our world must be and remain the way it is.

2. The sceptical solution is the one that Hume proposed in response to his own question. His response can be broken down into two parts:

a) Hume begins by rejecting every metaphysical solution to the problem of causality – it is impossible, he insists, to establish the future stability of natural laws by any sort of *a priori* reasoning. According to Hume, we have only two means at our disposal when it comes to establishing the truth of an existence or non-existence – experience and the principle of non-contradiction. But neither of these will allow us to demonstrate the necessity of the causal connection. For experience can only inform us about the present or the past, not the future. It may tell us that a law exists, or is susceptible to verification in the same way in which it has existed or been verified in the past, but it cannot establish that this law will continue to be verified in the future. As for the principle of non-contradiction, it allows us to establish *a priori*, and independently of any recourse to experience, that a contradictory event is impossible, that it cannot occur either today or tomorrow. But for Hume there is nothing contradictory in thinking that the same causes could produce different effects tomorrow.

Let us cite Hume's own illustration of his argument in Section IV of the *Enquiry Concerning Human Understanding*:

When I see, for instance, a Billiard-ball moving in a straight line towards another; even suppose motion in the second ball should by accident be suggested to me, as the result of their contact or impulse; may I not conceive, that a hundred different events might as well follow from that cause? May not both these balls remain at absolute rest? May not the first ball return in a straight line, or leap off from the second in any line or direction? All these suppositions are consistent and conceivable. Why then should we give the preference to one, which is no more consistent or conceivable than the rest? All our reasonings a priori will never be able to shew us any foundation for this preference. (Hume 1957: 44)

It is not just causal necessity, but what Leibniz called 'the principle of reason' that is being called into question here. We have seen how, according to such a principle, there must be a reason why everything is as it is rather than otherwise. But what Hume tells us is that such a reason is entirely inaccessible to thought, for since we cannot demonstrate that the laws must remain as they are, we cannot demonstrate the necessity of any fact – on the contrary, it would be perfectly compatible with the requirements of logic and experience for everything to become other than it is, whether natural processes, things, or events. There is no reason for anything to be or to remain self-identical.

b) But Hume is not content with disqualifying every possibility of a response to his question – he modifies the question itself in such a way as to replace it with a problem which does *admit of a solution*. Since we cannot demonstrate the necessity of the causal connection, he argues, we should stop asking ourselves why the laws are necessary and ask instead about the origin of our *belief* in their necessity. This amounts to a relocation of the problem that replaces a question about the nature of things with a question about our relation to things – one no longer asks why the laws are necessary, but why we are convinced that they are. Hume's answer to this question can be summed up in a single word: habit, or custom. When a fact recurs, it engenders in us a spontaneous feeling of habituation which gives rise to the certainty that the same thing will re-occur in the future. It is this propensity to believe that what has already recurred will invariably recur in the same way in the future that governs our entire relation to nature.

3. Lastly, the third type of response to Hume's problem is Kant's transcendental response – more precisely, the objective deduction of

the categories as elaborated in the *Critique of Pure Reason*'s 'Analytic of Concepts'. This deduction is certainly one of the most difficult sections of the *Critique*, but its basic principle is easy enough to grasp. We will briefly recapitulate it here, because we shall have occasion to return to it.

The transcendental solution differs from the classical metaphysical solution to the problem by substituting an *indirect* and *conditional* proof for a *direct* and *unconditional* one. We saw above how a metaphysical or dogmatic response to Hume's problem operated by producing a positive demonstration that there exists an absolutely necessary principle, then deriving the necessity of our world from it. By way of contrast, the transcendental enquiry produces an indirect proof of causal necessity, which is to say, a proof by *reductio ad absurdum*. It proceeds as follows: we begin by assuming that there is no causal necessity, and then we examine what ensues. But what ensues, according to Kant, is the complete destruction of every form of representation, for the resulting disorder among phenomena would be such as to preclude the lasting subsistence of any sort of objectivity and even of any sort of consciousness. Consequently, Kant considers the hypothesis of the contingency of the laws of nature to be refuted by the mere *fact* of representation. This is the regard in which Kant's response is conditional – he does not say that it is absolutely impossible that causality could cease to govern the world in the future; he merely says that it would be impossible for such an occurrence to *manifest itself* to consciousness – and this because if causality ceased to govern the world, everything would become devoid of consistency, and hence nothing would be representable. This is why Hume's imaginary scenario of the billiard-balls is impossible – for in this scenario, it is only the billiard-balls that escape causality, not the table upon which they roll, or the hall containing the table. It is precisely because the context remains stable that we are still able to *represent* something to ourselves when we imagine the fantastical possibilities suggested by Hume. However, says Kant, if representation were no longer structured by causality (along with the other categories of the understanding), it would no longer structure any aspect of the phenomenon at all, and nothing would remain, whether in the subject or the object, capable of sustaining our contemplation of it as spectators. Thus, causal necessity is a necessary condition for the existence of consciousness and the world it experiences. In other words, it is not absolutely necessary that causality governs all things, but *if* consciousness exists, then this can only be because there is a causality that necessarily governs phenomena.

For all their apparent differences, all three of these responses to Hume's problem share a common assumption. What they all have in common is the fact that none of them ever calls into question *the truth of the causal necessity*. In all three cases, the question is never whether causal necessity actually exists or not but rather whether or not it is possible to furnish a reason for its necessity. The self-evidence of this necessity is never called into question. This is obvious in the case of the metaphysical and the transcendental solutions, since they both proceed by trying to demonstrate its truth, but what is less obvious is that Hume too never really doubts causal necessity – he merely doubts our capacity to ground the latter through reasoning. For Hume, the 'ultimate cause of any natural operation'[3] must remain unknown to us – we may well be able to reduce the principles that underlie natural phenomena to a few general causes; nevertheless, Hume insists, 'as to the causes of these general causes, we should in vain attempt their discovery [...] These ultimate springs and principles are totally shut up from human curiosity and enquiry.'[4] In other words, we may well be able to uncover the basic laws that govern the universe – but the cause that underlies those laws themselves, and which endows them with necessity, will remain inaccessible to us. This is to concede that physical processes are indeed possessed of ultimate necessity. And it is precisely because Hume concedes this that he can characterize his own position as *sceptical* – for to be a sceptic is to concede that reason is incapable of providing a basis for our adherence to a necessity we assume to be real.

Our own speculative position refuses this assumption which all three of the aforementioned solutions share, in order to finally take seriously what the Humean – not Kantian – *a priori* teaches us about the world, viz., that *the same cause may actually bring about 'a hundred different events'* (and even many more). What Hume tells us is that *a priori*, which is to say from a purely logical point of view, any cause may actually produce any effect whatsoever, provided the latter is not contradictory. There can be no doubt that this is the evident lesson of reason, which is to say, of the thinking whose only fealty is to the requirements of logical intelligibility – reason informs us of the possibility that our billiard-balls might frolic about in a thousand different ways (and many more) on the billiard-table, without there being either a cause or a reason for this behaviour. For if reason knows of no *a prioris* other than that of non-contradiction, then it is perfectly compatible with reason for any consistent possibility to arise, without there being a discriminatory principle that would favour one possibility over another. Accordingly, it seems strange to begin by recusing the viewpoint of reason as obviously illusory, and then to attempt to provide a rational foundation for this recusal, or to conclude that the latter cannot be rationally supported. How could reason, for which the obvious falsity of causal necessity is blindingly evident, work against itself by demonstrating the truth of such a necessity? It is our senses that impose this belief in causality upon us, not thought. Thus, it would seem that a more judicious approach to the problem of the causal connection would begin on the basis of the evident falsity of this connection, rather than on the basis of its supposed truth. In any case, it is astonishing to note how in this matter, philosophers, who are generally the partisans of thought rather than of the senses, have opted overwhelmingly to trust their habitual perceptions, rather than the luminous clarity of intellection.

The sceptical position is the most paradoxical, for on the one hand it seeks to show how the principle of reason is incapable of founding its ontological pretensions, yet on the other, it continues to believe in the necessity – the real, physical necessity – that this principle has *injected* into the world. Although Hume no longer believes in metaphysics, he continues to believe in the necessity that metaphysics has extrapolated into things. Coupled with the unthinking propensity to believe in whatever recurs, this incomplete rejection of metaphysics results in a merely organic adherence to the phantasmatic world of metaphysics. Hume believes blindly in the world that metaphysicians thought they could prove. Thus, we should not be surprised at the ease with which such scepticism turns into superstition, for to assert and believe that there is an unfathomable necessity to the way of the world is to be prepared to believe in a great deal of providence. It seems to us that it would be wiser to believe in reason, and thereby to purge reality of the hinter-world of causal necessity.

We can now see in what regard the speculative position eliminates the contradictions usually attending Hume's problem. From our point of view, if the necessity of the causal connection cannot be demonstrated, then this is simply because the causal connection is devoid of necessity. But this is not to say that the speculative position eliminates every difficulty. For in fact we are going to *reformulate* Hume's problem in such a way as to shift its difficulty elsewhere. This reformulation can be stated as follows: instead of asking how we might demonstrate the supposedly genuine necessity of physical laws, *we must ask how we are to explain the*

manifest stability of physical laws given that we take these to be contingent.
Once reformulated, Hume's question is in fact the one we raised earlier: if
laws are contingent, and not necessary, then how is it that their contingency does not manifest itself in sudden and continual transformations?
How could laws for which there is no permanent foundation give rise to
a stable world? Our wager is that this formulation of the problem, unlike
its canonical version, allows of a satisfactory solution which requires no
limitation of the capacities of rationality.

For the reader who finds it decidedly difficult to concede that laws
could actually be contingent, perhaps the following analogy will help.
We are all familiar with the 'adventure' that gave birth to non-Euclidean
geometries: in order to prove Euclid's postulate that there is exactly one
parallel to a right angle from a given point, Lobachevsky assumed that this
thesis is false, and that it is possible to draw infinitely many lines through
the point that are all parallel to the original line. He did so assuming it
would lead to a contradiction, which would result in a proof by *reductio* of
Euclid's postulate. But instead of such a proof, Lobachevsky discovered a
new geometry, which is just as consistent as that of Euclid, but differs from
it. Perhaps those who are reluctant to accept the thesis we are proposing
might be willing to countenance the following suggestion: let us suppose
we are convinced of the necessity of the causal connection, but do not
believe in the possibility of providing a metaphysical demonstration of
its necessity – could we not attempt a proof by *reductio* of the actuality of
the causal connection? Could we not cancel this necessity in thought and
see if it does indeed lead us into absurdity? If it does, we will have proved
apagogically what we tried in vain to prove by invoking a metaphysical
principle of uniformity. But our wager is that what happened to those
geometers in the case of Euclid's postulate will also happen to us – little
by little, we will discover that the acausal universe is just as consistent
and just as capable of accounting for our actual experience as the causal
universe. But we will also discover that the former is a universe devoid
of all those enigmas that are part and parcel of the belief in physical
necessity. In other words, we have nothing to lose by moving from a
causal to an acausal universe – nothing except enigmas.

But it is immediately apparent that such an approach is going
to conflict fundamentally with the transcendental solution to Hume's
problem. For as we saw above, the transcendental deduction uses an
argument by *reductio* in order to infer from the absence of causal necessity
the destruction of representation. Our claim, on the contrary, is that

the hypothetical suspension of causal necessity does not necessarily entail consequences that are incompatible with the conditions of representation. Accordingly, our problem can be rendered still more precise: in order to establish the validity of our speculative solution to Hume's problem, we must expose the nature of the logical fallacy inherent in the transcendental deduction, so as to show, contrary to what the latter maintains, that the constancy of the phenomenal world does not amount to a refutation of the contingency of physical laws. In other words, we must show why it is a mistake to infer, as Kant does, the destruction of representation from the non-necessity of laws.

***

For Kant, if our representations of the world were not governed by necessary connections – which he calls the 'categories', among which is the principle of causality – the world would be nothing but a disordered mass of confused perceptions, incapable of yielding the experience of a unified consciousness. Thus, according to Kant, the very idea of consciousness and experience requires a structuring of representation capable of making our world into something other than a purely arbitrary sequence of disconnected impressions. This is the central thesis of the so-called 'objective' deduction of the categories, the aim of which is to legitimate the application of the categories to experience (the categories being understood as those universal connections presupposed by physics in particular). There can be no consciousness without the possibility of a science of phenomena, because the very idea of consciousness presupposes the idea of a representation that is unified in time.[5] But if the world was not governed by necessary laws, it would break up into experiences without coherence or succession, from whence no consciousness in the strict sense of the word could issue. Accordingly, the necessity of laws becomes an incontrovertible fact once one has construed it as the very condition for consciousness.

No doubt, we can only acknowledge the seemingly irrefutable character of this 'conditioning' argument – but this acknowledgement must be immediately qualified with the observation that it is only irrefutable insofar as it applies to the notion of *stability*, rather than to that of *necessity*. For the only incontrovertible – but also tautological – claim that can be unreservedly accorded to Kant is that the stability of phenomena provides the condition for consciousness as well as for a science of nature. Both the fact of this stability and its status as condition for science are obviously incontestable. But the same cannot be said of the inference –

which we will henceforth call 'the necessitarian inference' – underlying the claim that *the stability of laws presupposes, as its imperative condition, the necessity of those laws*. What we must now examine are the structure and assumptions underlying this inference.

Why does the incontestable fact of the stability of the laws of nature, which is to say, the exceptionless stability of nature's principle of uniformity, lead us to infer the necessity of this uniformity? By what reasoning do we move from the fact of stability – which is indeed general insofar as it has yet to be undermined – to an ontological necessity? The 'necessitarian' inference that underlies this reasoning can be broken down into three steps:

1. If the laws could actually change without reason – i.e. if they were not necessary – they would *frequently* change for no reason.
2. But the laws do not frequently change for no reason.
3. Consequently, the laws *cannot* change for no reason – in other words, they are necessary.

No one can contest proposition 2, which simply states the fact of the (manifest) stability of nature. Accordingly, the brunt of our evaluation of this inference must bear upon an assessment of implication 1, for if this implication turned out to be 'falsifiable', then the inference itself would collapse as a result of the disqualification of one of its premises. This implication proceeds from the *contingency* of laws – which is to say, from the possibility of their alteration – to the *actual frequency* of their alteration. This is why we will refer to it as the 'frequentialist implication' – for only if one accepts the validity of the implication that proceeds from the possibility of change to its frequency, can one accept the validity of the 'necessitarian' inference. In order to expose the invalidity of this latter inference, it is both necessary and sufficient to establish in what regard, and under what precise conditions, it becomes possible to reject the former implication.

First of all, it is important to note that the frequentialist implication not only underlies the Kantian argument in favour of causal necessity, but also the common belief in this necessity. To assert, as common opinion does, that if the laws of nature were contingent, 'we would have noticed', or to assert, as Kant does, that we would have noticed it to such an extent that we would know nothing, is in either case to maintain that the contingency of laws would entail an alteration of natural laws frequent enough to be manifested in experience, or even to destroy the very possibility of experience. Both theses, the common thesis and the Kantian thesis, rely on the same argument – viz., that contingency implies frequent transformation – differing only with regard to the intensity of the frequency which they infer from contingency (for the common thesis, the frequency would be low but manifest, while for the Kantian thesis, the frequency would be so high as to destroy representation). We must pause and take a closer look at this implication, and try to understand why it seems so obvious that Kant executes it without even bothering to justify it – something that could also be said of common sense and of the majority of the partisans of physical necessity.

We are aided in this task by Jean-René Vernes' *Critique of Aleatory Reason*, which provides us with a valuable resource.[6] The chief merit of this brief essay, written with a concision worthy of the philosophers of the seventeenth century, lies in the way in which it exposes the reasoning upon which both Hume and Kant implicitly rely when they assume that the necessity of laws is obvious. But it is important to point out right away that for Vernes this reasoning is *legitimate* – thus, he holds the belief in the necessity of physical laws to be well-founded. Vernes' project consists in rendering explicit the reasoning that is implicit in Hume and Kant, the better to underline the sense in which it is true. By way of contrast, the relevance of Vernes' thesis for us is that by excavating this reasoning and exposing its true nature, he allows us to discover its weak-point.

Vernes' thesis is the following: the inference whereby we proceed implicitly from the stability of laws to their necessity consists in a piece of *probabilistic* reasoning – 'probabilistic' in the *mathematical* sense of the term. Recall Hume's text about the billiard-balls, which we cited above. According to Vernes, this text harbours both the (explicit) root of the problem of causality, and the (unnoticed) key to its rational solution. What lies at the root of the problem? The fact that there is a massive difference between the *a priori* or 'imaginary' possibilities – more generally, all those possibilities that are conceivable (non-contradictory) – and those possibilities that are actually *experienced*. Contrary to Kant's identification of the *a priori* with necessity and of the empirical realm with contingency, for Vernes it is the *a priori* that presents us with contingency, while it is experience that presents us with necessity. The enigma resides in the fact that *a priori* 'a hundred different events' as Hume says – or even, as Vernes puts it, 'a practically infinite number'[7] of different events – could arise from the same series of causes, *ceteris paribus*. Thus, *a priori*, the balls might behave in thousands upon thousands of different ways, whereas in experience, only one of those possibilities is effectuated each time – the possibility that conforms to the physical law of impacts.

But by what right then do we conclude from this difference between the *a priori* and the experiential that it is the *a priori* that is deceptive, and not experience that is illusory? What is it that allows us to claim that the constancy of experience opens onto a genuine necessity, whereas the *a priori* does not open onto a veritable contingency? The answer is that our assumption in this case is exactly the same as that which would lead a gambler to suspect (at the very least) that a die that always lands the same face up is *very probably* loaded. Let us take a set of events configured in such a way that there is *a priori no reason* why any one of them should occur *rather than* any other. This would be the case for a set of dice, both of which we assume to be perfectly homogeneous and symmetrical, and about which we can assume *a priori* that there is no reason for any one of their faces to turn up more frequently than any other given an unbiased throw. When, armed with this hypothesis, we attempt to calculate the likelihood of one event occurring (understood as this or that outcome of throwing the dice), we implicitly assume the following *a priori* principle: *whatever is equally thinkable is equally possible*. It is precisely this *quantitative* equality between the thinkable and the possible that allows us to work out the probability or frequency of an event when we play a game of chance – given that, in the kinds of circumstances outlined above, one of two events has no more (this 'more' being strictly mathematical) reason to occur than the other (whether as the result of throwing the dice, or of tossing a coin, or of spinning a roulette wheel, etc.), then we must assume that each has as much chance of actually occurring as the other, and use this assumption to arrive at calculable estimations as to the probability of complex events entirely composed of this initial equi-probability (such as the chance of the dice turning up a double-six, or of the roulette wheel turning up 0 three times in row, etc.).

But now let us suppose that the dice with which we have been playing for an hour have continually been landing with the same face up. We would say to ourselves, invoking the principle according to which events that are equally possible are equally probable, that there is only a very small likelihood that this is the result of genuine chance. There must be *a cause* (perhaps a lead ball hidden in the dice) *necessitating this single result*. But let us now suppose that the dice we are playing with have been landing with the same face up not just for an hour, but throughout our entire lives, and even as far back as human memory stretches. And let us also suppose that these dice are not just six-sided, but possess millions and millions of sides. We now find ourselves in the same situation as Hume pondering his billiard-balls – for each event given in experience, we can conceive *a priori* of a great many different empirical outcomes (indeed, a number so immense it seems vain to try to determine it), all of which appear to us to be equally possible. Yet we continue to obtain the same outcome, which is to say, the same effects from the same causes. Thus, when Hume or Kant assume that the necessity of laws is self-evident, their reasoning is exactly the same as that of the gambler faced with loaded dice, because they implicitly assume the validity of the inference unearthed by Vernes, viz., that if physical laws were actually contingent, it would be contrary to the laws that govern chance if this contingency had never manifested itself. Consequently, *there must be* a necessitating reason, albeit hidden – just as there must be a lead ball imbedded in the dice – that explains the invariance in the result.

The implicit principle governing the necessitarian inference now becomes clear: the latter proceeds by *extending the probabilistic reasoning* which the gambler applied to an event that is *internal* to our universe (the throw of the dice and its result), to *the universe as such*. This reasoning can be reconstructed as follows: I construe our own physical universe as one among an immense number of conceivable (i.e. non-contradictory) universes each governed by different sets of physical laws; universes in which the impact of two billiard-balls does not conform to the laws that govern our own universe but results rather in both balls flying off into the air, or fusing together, or turning into two immaculate but rather grumpy mares, or into two maroon but rather affable lilies, etc. Thus, I mentally construct a 'dice-universe' which I identify with the *Universe of all universes*, bound globally by the principle of non-contradiction alone, each face of which constitutes a single universe governed by a determinate set of physical laws. Then, for any situation given in experience, I roll these dice in my mind (I envisage all the conceivable consequences of this event), yet in the end, I find that the same result (given the same circumstances) always occurs: the dice-universe always lands with the face representing 'my' universe up, and the laws of impact are never violated. Every time it is thrown, this dice-universe invariably results in the same physical universe – mine, the one I have always been able to observe on a daily basis. No doubt, theoretical physics will always be able to teach me new and expected things about the particular face-universe I inhabit – but this will simply amount to a deeper knowledge of my universe, rather than to an aleatory transformation of the universe itself. The latter has never infringed the principle of uniformity; it has always presented me with the same result given the same initial conditions. The improbability of this stability in the outcome seems so aberrant that I do not even pause to consider the possibility that it might be solely the result of chance. Consequently, I infer from it – via an inference which is generally executed too quickly even to be noticed – the existence of a *necessary* reason, but a necessity that is *extra-logical* as well as *extra-mathematical*. This necessity provides the ineliminable supplement to the argumentative necessity of logico-mathematical reasoning, since the latter presents me with a dice-universe that is *homogeneous* – in other words, each face of which is *equally conceivable*. Thus, I redouble the necessity proper to logico-mathematical notation with a *second type of necessity*, a real or physical necessity, which alone – like the lead ball imbedded in the dice – is capable of furnishing the reason for the obvious 'fixing' of the outcome. It is then entirely up to me whether to call the source of this second necessity 'matter' (as Vernes does) or 'providence' – whatever I choose to call it, it will remain a primordial and enigmatic fact.

To sum up: the Humean-Kantian inference is an instance of proba-bilistic reasoning applied not to an event in our universe, but rather to our universe itself considered as merely one among a totality of possible universes. The nub of the argument consists in registering the immense numerical gap between those possibilities that are conceivable and those that are actually experienced, in such a way as to derive from this gap the following probabilistic aberration (which provides the source for the frequentialist implication): if physical laws *could actually change for no reason*, it would be extraordinarily improbable if they did not change *frequently*, not to say frenetically. Indeed, they would change so frequently that we would have to say – and here we move from Hume to Kant – not just that we would have noticed it already, but that we would never have been here to notice it in the first place, since the ensuing chaos would have precluded the minimal degree of order and continuity required for the correlation between consciousness and world. Thus, necessity is proven by a fact of immensely improbable stability, viz., the permanence of the laws of nature, and by the subjective obverse of this permanence, which is the consciousness of a subject capable of science. Such is the logic of the necessitarian argument, and more particularly, of the frequentialist implication that underlies it.

***

Before we proceed to outline the speculative refutation of the necessitarian argument, it is necessary to note that there is a well known
rejoinder to such an argument, and it consists in demonstrating that the
continuing existence of our world can in fact be explained by chance
alone. It proceeds in the same way as the Epicureans explained the apparently purposeful existence of living beings – one compares the emergence
of the most complex organisms to another, suitably improbable outcome
(such as, for example, writing the *Iliad* by randomly throwing letters at
a given surface), before pointing out that even this outcome ceases to be
anomalous given a sufficiently gigantic number of attempts. Similarly, one
response to the aforementioned probabilistic objection would be to point
out that our own highly structured world could have been the result of a
gigantic number of chaotic emergences that finally stabilized themselves
in the configuration of our universe.

Yet this response to the necessitarian argument cannot satisfy us;
and this for the very simple reason that it continues to presuppose
the necessity of physical laws. Thus, it is important to notice that the
very notion of chance is only conceivable on condition that there are
unalterable physical laws. This is precisely what the example of the dice-
throw shows: an aleatory sequence can only be generated on condition
that the dice preserve their structure from one throw to the next, and that
the laws allowing the throw to be carried out not change from one cast
to the next. If from one throw to the next the dice imploded, or became
flat or spherical, or if gravity ceased to operate and they flew off into
the air, or on the contrary, were projected underground, etc., then there
would be no aleatory sequence, and it would be impossible to establish
a calculus of probabilities. Thus chance always presupposes some form
of physical invariance – far from permitting us to think the contingency
of physical laws, chance itself is nothing other than a certain type of
physical law – one that is 'indeterministic'. In Epicurus for instance, it
is clear that the *clinamen*, the tiny aleatory deviation in the trajectory of
atoms, presupposes the immutability of physical laws: the specific shape
of atoms (smooth, hooked, etc.), the number of different kinds of atoms,
the indivisible character of these elementary physical units, the existence
of the void, etc. – none of these can ever be modified by the *clinamen*
itself, since they provide the conditions for its effectuation.

But our response to the necessitarian objection must allow us to
conceive of a world devoid of *any* physical necessity that would still be

compatible with the fact of the stability of laws. Accordingly, we must deploy an argument that does not at any point redouble the purely logical necessity of non-contradiction (which we derived from the principle of factiality, and which is the only necessity that is recognized as true *a priori* by Hume) with a real necessity, which is to say, with a necessity that would install a *principle of preference* between equally conceivable options. Yet it is precisely such a principle of preference that the aleatory response to the necessitarian objection introduces, since there is no contradiction involved in thinking a modification in the determinate conditions that allow a random process to be carried out (for example: a modification in the form of the dice, or in their number of faces, or in the laws that govern their throws, etc.). Moreover, such a response would not convince anyone, for it concedes to the objector the notion that we have up until now benefited from a favourable draw, and hence from a *luck* that might well turn, incessantly producing different outcomes. We would then be plunged into that relation to the world which we earlier qualified as absurd, and which would incite us to fear at every moment the random behaviour of reality.

Thus, the refutation of the frequential implication cannot consist in demonstrating that the stability of the world conforms to the laws of chance – rather, it should demonstrate that the contingency of natural laws remains *inaccessible to aleatory reasoning*. Contrary to responses of the Epicurean type, we should not grant the legitimacy of our opponent's reasoning, and then try to render it compatible with actual experience. Instead, we must disqualify this reasoning as such by showing that it makes inappropriate use of the categories of chance and probability, outside their legitimate field of application. In other words, we must show that one cannot apply these categories to the laws of the physical world as such, and that the use of probabilistic reasoning in such a context is meaningless. We will then have succeeded in showing how the stability of laws is compatible with their absolute contingency, and we will have done so apparently contrary to all 'healthy probability'. We will also have done so by disqualifying the absurd fear of continual disorder, since this fear relies precisely on the aleatory conception of physical laws that encourages us to interpret the actual stability of representations as an extraordinary piece of luck. In other words, we must elaborate a concept of the *contingency* of laws that is fundamentally distinct from the concept of *chance*.

Yet it would certainly be possible to establish this difference between the two notions solely with the help of the preceding remark about chance, which is to say, by maintaining that the contingency of laws should not be confused with chance, since the effectuation of the latter already presupposes a pre-existing set of laws. We could then maintain that the contingency of laws cannot be subjected to the categories of chance, since such contingency is capable of affecting the very conditions that allow chance events to occur and exist. We would thereby disqualify the frequentialist implication that reasons about laws as if they were the result of an aleatory throw, failing to see that it is precisely such laws that provide the condition for the throw. However, even if it is not fundamentally incorrect, such a response on our part would be disappointing. It would confine itself to safeguarding contingency from a specific objection, without attempting to *deepen* its concept. We would confine ourselves to saying what contingency is not (i.e. chance), without taking advantage of the necessitarian objection as an opportunity for stating more precisely what it is. But factial ontology is not intended to be a 'negative ontology' – we do not wish to confine ourselves to maintaining that contingency as we understand it is not accessible to this or that type of reasoning; rather, our aim is to elaborate an ever more determinate, ever richer concept of contingency. Accordingly, every difficulty encountered by factial speculation should be converted into a means for identifying a *determinate condition of chaos* capable of allowing us to overcome the obstacle. This is the basic principle of a reason that has been emancipated from the principle of reason – its progressive unfolding demands that we exhibit the positive and differentiated properties of the absence of reason. Thus, a genuinely satisfactory speculative resolution of Hume's problem should explain what could constitute *a precise condition for the manifest stability of chaos*. This condition would allow us to penetrate more deeply into the nature of a temporality delivered from real necessity. But as we are about to see, such a condition exists, and it is *mathematical* in nature: it is the *transfinite*.

***

In order to counter the frequentialist implication, we must begin by identifying its fundamental ontological presupposition. For in fact, this implication holds only in a very particular case, and on condition of a singularly strong ontological hypothesis, because it conjoins the being of the possible and the being of the Whole. Thus, this probabilistic reasoning is only valid on condition that what is *a priori* possible be thinkable in terms of a numerical totality.

Granted, the frequentialist implication does not have to provide a precise determination of the cardinality of conceivable possibilities in order to 'work' and to remain legitimate – the greater the number by which the conceivable possibilities exceed the number of actually experienced possibilities, the greater the extent of the probabilistic anomaly, and it is obvious that there are in any case immensely more conceivable possibilities than experienced ones. It does not even really matter whether this totality of possibilities is finite or infinite, since the infinite is no obstacle to the application of probabilities. Any object, even one directly given in experience, can provide me with the opportunity for a probabilistic calculation on the infinite. This infinity, which is tied to the continuity of the object under consideration, does not preclude the possibility of carrying out a positive evaluation of the sought-for event. Take for example a homogeneous rope of determinate length, both of whose extremities are being subjected to equal tension. I can calculate the positive probability that it will break at one of its points, even though these 'breaking points' are theoretically infinite in number along the length of the rope, since they are 'dimensionless'. Moreover, I can do so despite the apparent paradox, according to which, since the probability of any one of these 'dimensionless' points being the breaking point is one over infinity, the rope is incapable of breaking at any of its points. Yet all that is necessary to obviate this 'paradox' is to select a segment of rope, however small, and probability once more becomes applicable to the latter as efficiently as in those cases where the number of possibilities is a natural whole number.[8]

Thus, all that is required for the frequentialist implication to work is the assumption that there does indeed exist a totality of non-contradictory conceivable possibilities, and the stipulation that this totality, whatever its cardinality, is immensely larger than the set of physically possible events. But this is to say that in order for the inference to be legitimate, there is one uncircumventable condition that must be satisfied, viz., *that there is a totality of conceivable possibilities*. It is necessary to assume that a set of possible worlds (the 'dice-universe' we invoked earlier) is actually conceivable, if not intuitable, within which we can then carry out our extension of probabilistic reasoning from objects that are *internal* to our universe (the dice, the rope) to the universe *as such*. Thus, probabilistic reasoning is conceivable on condition that it be possible to conceive a totality of cases within which one can then calculate frequencies by determining the ratio of the number of favourable cases to the number of possible cases. If you revoke the notion of a set of cases and the idea of a total-universe from whence the events submitted to analysis are drawn, then aleatory reasoning becomes meaningless.

Accordingly, aleatory reasoning – which is to say, the very idea of chance insofar as the latter is subject to a calculus of frequency – presupposes the notion of numerical totality. When totality is internal to our universe, then it is either directly given to us in experience (as in the case of the number of faces of the dice, or the number of segments of the cord), or indirectly, via an observation of the frequency of a given phenomenon. But when I attempt to apply probabilistic reasoning to our universe as a whole, I assume – without there being anything in experience that could validate this assumption – that it is legitimate to consider the conceivable as another instance of a totality of cases. Thus, I subject the conceivable to a mathematical hypothesis: I turn it into a set, however large. I turn it into the set of possible worlds because I consider it *a priori* legitimate to think the possible as a Whole.

But it is precisely this totalization of the thinkable which can *no longer* be guaranteed *a priori*. For we now know – indeed, we have known it at least since Cantor's revolutionary set-theory – that we have no grounds for maintaining that the conceivable is *necessarily* totalizable. For one of the fundamental components of this revolution was the *detotalization of number*, a detotalization also known as *'the transfinite'*.

On this particular point, it is the signal work of Alain Badiou – and primarily *Being and Event*[9] – that has been decisive for us. Among Badiou's fundamental theses is the one whereby he maintains – through his own prescriptions – the ontological pertinence of Cantor's theorem, in such a way as to reveal *the mathematical conceivability of the detotalization of being-qua-being*. Although our interpretation of the ontological scope of this detotalization is not the same as Badiou's, it is thanks to his singular project that we have been able to discover the means through which to extricate ourselves from the ontological conditions inherent in the necessitarian inference. For one of the most forceful aspects of *Being and Event* resides in the way in which it uses mathematics itself to effect a liberation from the limits of calculatory reason, a gesture altogether more powerful than any external critique of calculation in the name of some supposedly superior register of philosophical thought. In this regard, as well as through many other aspects of his thought, Alain Badiou has carried out a profound reinvestment of the inaugural decisions of philosophy as such, for there is no fundamental episode in philosophy since Plato that has not proceeded via a re-interpretation of its originary alliance with mathematics. Moreover, he has also, we believe, summoned each of us to try to grasp anew the meaning of this privileged link between these two discourses.

For our part, and to begin with, we have attempted to remain faithful to this gesture through the following thesis: there is a mathematical way of rigorously distinguishing contingency from chance, and it is provided by the transfinite.

In order to be as concise and as clear as possible about the issue of the transfinite, we can put things in the following way:[10] one of the most remarkable aspects of the standard axiomatization of set-theory (known as 'ZF', for 'Zermelo-Fraenkel'), progressively elaborated during the first half of the twentieth century on the basis of Cantor's work, consists in its unencompassable pluralization of infinite quantities. 'Cantor's theorem', as it is known, can be intuitively glossed as follows: take any set, count its elements, then compare this number to the number of possible groupings of these elements (by two, by three – but there are also groupings 'by one', or 'by all', which is identical with the whole set). You will always obtain the same result: the set B of possible groupings (or parts) of a set A is always bigger than A – *even if A is infinite*.[11] It is possible to construct an unlimited succession of infinite sets, each of which is of a quantity superior to that of the set whose parts it collects together. This succession is known as the series of alephs, or the series of transfinite cardinals. But this series itself *cannot be totalized*, in other words, it cannot be collected together into some 'ultimate' quantity. For it is clear that were such a quantitative totalization to exist, then it would also have to allow itself to be surpassed in accordance with the procedure of the grouping of parts. Thus, the set T (for Totality) of all quantities cannot 'contain' the quantity obtained by the set of the parts of T. Consequently, this 'quantity of all quantities' is not construed as being 'too big' to be grasped by thought – it is simply construed as not existing. Within the standard set-theoretical axiomatic, that which is quantifiable, and even more generally, that which is thinkable – which is to say, sets in general, or whatever can be constructed or demonstrated in accordance with the requirement of consistency – does not constitute a totality. For this totality of the thinkable is itself logically inconceivable, since it gives rise to a contradiction. We will retain the following translation of Cantor's transfinite: *the (quantifiable) totality of the thinkable is unthinkable*.

Accordingly, the strategy for resolving Hume's problem can now be stated in the following way.

We are not claiming that the non-totalizing axiomatic is the only possible (i.e. thinkable) one. Consequently, we are not claiming that the possible is always untotalizable, even if this is the case in the standard axiomatic of sets. For we cannot deny *a priori* the possibility that it could also be thinkable that the thinkable constitutes a totality. The fact that the untotalizable is thinkable within a given axiomatic does not prevent anyone from choosing another axiomatic, in which the frequentialist implication would still be valid. There is always more than one axiomatic, and despite its eminence, that of standard set-theory is only one among many. Thus, we cannot rule out *a priori* the possibility of selecting an axiomatic in which the realm of possible worlds would constitute an ultimate and determinate numerical totality. But this at least must be accorded to us: we have at our disposal *one* axiomatic capable of providing us with the resources for thinking that the possible is untotalizable. However, the mere fact that we are able to assume the truth of this axiomatic enables us to disqualify the necessitarian inference, and with it every reason for continuing to believe in the existence of the necessity of physical laws – a necessity that is mysteriously superimposed onto the fact of the stability of these same laws.

What the set-theoretical axiomatic demonstrates is at the very least a fundamental uncertainty regarding the totalizability of the possible. But this uncertainty alone enables us to carry out a decisive critique of the necessitarian inference by destroying one of the latter's fundamental postulates: we can only move immediately from the stability of laws to their necessity so long as we do not question the notion that the possible is *a priori* totalizable. But since this totalization is at best only operative within certain axiomatics, rather than in all of them, we can no longer continue to claim that the frequentialist implication is absolutely valid. We have no way of knowing whether the possible can be totalized in the same way as the faces of a set of dice can be totalized. This ignorance suffices to expose *the illegitimacy of extending aleatory reasoning beyond a totality that is already given in experience*. Since we cannot decide *a priori* (i.e. through the use of logical-mathematical procedures alone) whether or not a totality of the possible exists, then we should restrict the claims of aleatory reasoning solely to objects of experience, rather than extending it – as Kant implicitly does in his objective deduction – to the very laws that govern our universe, as if we knew that the latter necessarily belongs to some greater Whole. Since both theses (viz., that the possible is numerically totalizable, and that it is not) are *a priori* conceivable, only experience can provide us with an assurance as to the validity of aleatory reasoning, by acting as guarantor for the actual existence of the totality which is required in order for that reasoning to work – whether in the form of a direct experience of a supposedly homogeneous object (e.g. the dice or the rope), or in the form of a statistical analysis (determination of average values and of appropriate frequencies for an identifiable phenomenon). Accordingly, the only totalities available to us that are capable of legitimating this type of aleatory reasoning must be given to us *within our universe* – which is to say, experientially. Kant's belief in the necessity of laws is thereby revoked as an instance of aleatory reason's unwarranted pretension to reach beyond the limits of experience.

For it is in fact this illegitimate application of probabilities beyond the limits of our experience that allows Kant, at several junctures in the 1st Critique, to derive from the hypothesis of the contingency of laws, the necessity of their frequent modification. Thus, in the following passage, the inference from the possibility of contingency to the necessary frequency of its effectuation is particularly evident:

> Unity of synthesis according to empirical concepts [which in this context means primarily the application of the relation of causality to phenomena – QM] *would be altogether contingent*, if these latter were not based on a transcendental ground of unity. Otherwise, *it would be possible for appearances to crowd in upon the soul, and yet to be such as would never allow of experience*. Since connection in accordance with universal and necessary laws would be lacking, all relation of knowledge to objects would fall away. The appearances might indeed constitute intuition without thought, but not knowledge, and consequently would be for us as good as nothing. (Kant 1929: 138, A111 – my emphasis)[12]

Kant infers from the assumption of the actual contingency of phenomenal laws modifications of reality so extreme that they would necessarily entail the destruction of the very possibility of knowledge, and even of consciousness. But how is Kant able to determine the *actual frequency* of the modification of laws, assuming the latter to be contingent? How does he know that this frequency would be so *extraordinarily significant* as to destroy the very possibility of science, and even of consciousness? By what right does he rule out *a priori* the *possibility* that contingent laws might only very *rarely* change – so rarely indeed that no one would ever have had the opportunity to witness such a modification? It can only be by the right which he derives from applying the calculus of probability to our world as a whole, rather than to any phenomenon given within the world, and hence from an *a priori* totalization of the possible, which we know, since Cantor, can no longer lay claim to any logical or mathematical necessity – which is to say, to any sort of *a priori* necessity.[13]

***

What has been our approach to Hume's problem, and to what extent can we claim to have provided a solution to it?

We began by reformulating the problem: instead of assuming that Hume's imaginary hypothesis concerning 'a hundred different events' resulting from the same causal sequence was a chimera which had to be refuted, we sought to uncover what it was exactly that prevented us from believing in the truth of such a hypothesis, given that reason, on the contrary, issued an emphatic invitation to accept it. We then noticed that at the root of this presupposition lay an instance of probabilistic reasoning applied to the laws of nature themselves; a piece of reasoning which there was no reason to accept once its condition – the claim that conceivable possibilities constitute a totality – was revealed to be no more than a hypothesis, as opposed to an indubitable truth.

In doing so, although we have not positively demonstrated that the possible is untotalizable, we have identified an alternative between two options – viz., the possible either does or does not constitute a totality – with regard to which we have every reason to opt for the second – every reason, since it is precisely the second option that allows us to follow what reason indicates – viz., that there is no necessity to physical laws – without wasting further energy trying to resolve the enigmas inherent in the first option. For whoever totalizes the possible legitimates the frequential implication, and thereby the source of the belief in real necessity, the reason for which no one will ever be able to understand – thus, whoever does so must maintain *both* that physical laws are necessary *and* that no one can know why it is these laws, rather than others, which necessarily exist. But on the contrary, whoever detotalizes the possible is able to think the stability of laws without having to redouble them with an enigmatic physical necessity. Consequently, we can apply Ockham's razor to the hypothesis of real necessity: since the latter is an 'entity' that is superfluous for explaining the world, we can safely dispense with it without depriving ourselves of anything except for a mystery. Thus, the resolution of Hume's problem allows us to remove a fundamental obstacle to the complete embrace of the principle of factiality, because it rules out, as a henceforth familiar sophism, the transcendental objection which invariably infers an actual, random disorder of representations from the contingency of laws.

***

We know that the terms 'chance' (from the Vulgar Latin: *cadentia*) and 'aleatory' (from the Latin: *alea*) both refer back to related etymologies: 'to fall', and 'falling' in the case of the former; 'dice', 'dice-throw', or 'game of dice' in the case of the latter. Thus, these terms bring together notions that, far from being opposed to one another, are actually inseparable – the notions of play and of calculation, and of the calculation of chance which is inherent in every game of dice. Every thinking in which the identification of being with chance is dominant foregrounds the theme of the dice-totality (which is to say, of the unalterable enclosure of the number of the possible), of the apparent gratuity of the game (the play of life and of a world whose superior artificiality is acknowledged), but also that of the cool calculation of frequencies (the world of life insurance and evaluable risks). The ontology of the enclosure of possibilities inevitably situates us within a world whose aversion to gravity is but the obverse of the fact that it only takes counting techniques seriously.

By way of contrast, the term 'contingency' refers back to the Latin *contingere*, meaning 'to touch, to befall', which is to say, that which happens, but which happens enough to happen *to* us. The contingent, in a word, is *something that finally happens* – something other, something which, in its irreducibility to all pre-registered possibilities, puts an end to the vanity of a game wherein everything, even the improbable, is predictable. When something happens to us, when novelty grabs us by the throat, then no more calculation and no more play – it is time to be serious. But what is most fundamental in all this – and this was already one of the guiding intuitions of *Being and Event* – is the idea that the most powerful conception of the incalculable and unpredictable event is provided by a thinking that *continues to be* mathematical – rather than one which is artistic, poetic, or religious. It is *by way of* mathematics that we will finally succeed in thinking that which, through its power and beauty, vanquishes quantities and sounds the end of play.

***

In light of the foregoing, we can now grasp the general tenor of the factial approach. Our project can in fact be formulated as follows: our aim is to supplant the contemporary *dissolution* of metaphysical problems by a *non-metaphysical precipitation* of these same problems. Let us quickly explain what this supplanting entails.

What will be the reaction of many contemporary philosophers (albeit fewer and fewer) when confronted by Hume's problem, or by the question as to why there is something rather than nothing? Generally speaking, they will try to find the easiest way to shrug their shoulders. They will try to demonstrate to you that there is nothing enigmatic about your question, because it does not even need to be raised any more. Thus, they will endeavour, in a spirit of charity – tirelessly repeating the Duchampian-Wittgensteinian gesture – to make you understand that there is no enigma, because there is no problem. These philosophers will claim to have dissolved your 'naïve' problem – 'naïve' because metaphysical, dogmatic, etc. – by unveiling the (linguistic, historical) source of this vain questioning. Ultimately, what they are really interested in is finding out how it was possible (and how it is still possible – you, the questioner, being proof of it) to be perplexed by such 'pseudo-problems'.

The end of metaphysics is still largely identified with this type of dissolvent approach – it is no longer a matter of asking oneself metaphysical questions, since the latter are mere semblances of questions, or questions that are now irremediably obsolete, but rather of raising questions on, or about metaphysics. But we now know that the contemporary belief in the insolubility of metaphysical questions *is merely the consequence of the continuing belief in the principle of reason* – for only someone who continues to believe that to speculate is to seek out the ultimate reason for things being thus and so, also believes that there is no hope of resolving metaphysical questions. Only someone who believes that the essence of the answer to a metaphysical question lies in discovering a cause or a necessary reason can estimate, rightly, that these problems will never be resolved. This is a discourse of the limits of thought, which we now know to be a consequence of the *perpetuating denial* of metaphysics. Accordingly, we can now see that the veritable end of metaphysics is materialized by the attempt to extract from this dissolution the *precipitate* of these venerable questions, now restored to their sovereign legitimacy. For it is by resolving the questions of metaphysics that we become able to under-stand that the essence of the latter consisted in generating problems that it could not answer so long as it retained its fundamental postulate – only by abandoning the principle of reason can we begin to make sense of these problems.

Thus, the factial stance proceeds by abandoning the dissolvent approach to metaphysics as a procedure that has itself become obsolete. For the postulate of dissolution – viz., that metaphysical problems are not really problems, but false problems, pseudo-questions constituted in such a way that it makes no sense to assume they could ever admit of a solution – this postulate begins to crumble once we learn to renounce the principle of reason. As a result, metaphysical problems are revealed always to have been genuine problems, since they do admit of a solution. But their resolution depends on one precise and highly constraining condition – that we begin to understand that in reply to those metaphysical questions that ask why the world is thus and not otherwise, the response 'for no reason' is a genuine answer. Instead of laughing or smiling at questions like 'Where do we come from?', 'Why do we exist?', we should ponder instead the remarkable fact that the replies 'From nothing. For nothing' really *are* answers, thereby realizing that these really were questions – and excellent ones at that. There is no longer a mystery, not because there is no longer a problem, but because there is no longer a reason.

***

However, we must return to our proposed resolution of Hume's problem, for the former cannot wholly satisfy us. As we saw, this resolution is fundamentally non-Kantian insofar as it aims to establish the conceivability of the actual contingency of the laws of nature. Yet it would not be quite right to assert that our resolution itself is unequivocally speculative, just because it is anti-transcendental in intent. For although the thesis we advanced was ontological, and did indeed assert something about the in-itself rather than phenomena in maintaining the detotalization of the possible, nevertheless, it was only advanced as an ontological *hypothesis*. We have not established whether this non-totalization actually obtains, we have merely supposed it, and drawn the consequences of the fact that such a supposition is possible. In other words, although our proposed resolution of Hume's problem gives us grounds for not immediately giving up on the idea of factial speculation, it has not itself been engendered as a truth by means of speculative reasoning. For a properly factial resolution of Hume's problem would require that we derive the non-totalization of the possible *from the principle of factiality itself*. In order to elaborate such a solution, we would have to derive the non-whole as a figure of factiality, just as we sketched the derivation of consistency and of the 'there is'. This would entail absolutizing the transfinite in the same way in which we absolutized consistency – which is to say that we would have to think the former as an explicit condition of contingent-being, rather than merely construing it as a mathematically formulated hypothesis that can be advantageously supported by the speculative. But it is clear that such a resolution of the problem would require that we be in a position to do for mathematical necessity what we tried to do for logical necessity. We would have to be able to rediscover an in-itself that is Cartesian, and no longer just Kantian – in other words, we would have to be able to legitimate the absolute bearing of the mathematical – rather than merely logical – restitution of a reality that is construed as independent of the existence of thought. It would be a question of establishing that the possibilities of which chaos – which is the only in-itself – is actually capable cannot be measured by any number, whether finite or infinite, and that it is precisely this super-immensity of the chaotic virtual that allows the impeccable stability of the visible world.

But it is clear that such a derivation would not only have to be far more complex, but also more adventurous than that of consistency, since it would have to demonstrate how a specific mathematical theorem, and not just a general rule of the *logos*, is one of the absolute conditions of contingency. Accordingly, it might seem wiser to confine ourselves to our hypothetical resolution of Hume's problem, since the latter seems sufficient to vanquish the objection from physical stability, which provided the only 'rational' motive for not simply abandoning every variant of the principle of reason. However, there is *another* problem that rules out such caution, and it is precisely the problem of ancestrality. For as we saw, the resolution of the latter demanded an unequivocal demonstration of the *absoluteness* of mathematical discourse. We begin to see then, albeit dimly, that there now seem to be two problems tied to the issue of the absolute scope of mathematics – the problem of the arche-fossil and the problem of Hume. It remains for us to connect them in such a way as to provide a precise formulation of the task for non-metaphysical speculation.

Chapter 5
Ptolemy's Revenge

The problem of ancestrality, or of the arche-fossil, such as we described it in Chapter 1, bears upon the following general question: how are we to understand the meaning of scientific statements about a manifestation of the world which is supposed to be anterior to any human form of the relation to the world? Or again: how are we to conceive of the meaning of a discourse which construes the relation to the world, whether living and/or thinking, as a fact inscribed within a temporality in which this relation is merely one event among others – a fact situated in a sequence of which it is merely a stage, and not the origin? How is science even capable of conceiving such statements, and in what regard are we to attribute an eventual truth to them?

We must now try to render the formulation of this question more precise. Closer inspection reveals that the problem of the arche-fossil is not confined to ancestral statements. For it concerns every discourse whose meaning includes a *temporal discrepancy* between thinking and being – thus, not only statements about events occurring prior to the emergence of humans, but also statements about possible events that are *ulterior* to the extinction of the human species. For the same problem arises when we try to determine the conditions of meaning for hypotheses about the climactic and geological consequences of a meteor impact extinguishing all life on earth. We will use the term '*dia-chronicity*' to provide a general characterization of all such statements about events that are anterior or ulterior to every terrestrial-relation-to-the-world – the former expressing the temporal hiatus between world and relation-to-the-world that is inherent in the very meaning of such discourse. Accordingly, it is the conditions of meaning for dia-chronic statements in general that concern us.

But the latter does not only pertain to *certain* types of scientific statement, or only to a specific type of scientific research, such as could be restricted to the science of dating, for instance. For what is at stake in dia-chronicity is indeed the nature of empirical science *in general*. The problem of dia-chronicity is not just a function of the fact that science has actually established a temporal hiatus between being and terrestrial thought; it concerns the fact that *this is a possibility that was rendered meaningful by the very inception of modern science*. It is not the question of fact that we are concerned with – i.e. the fact that dia-chronic statements are verified or falsified – but rather the question of right or principle; that is to say, the question of the status of the discourse which renders the verification *or* falsification of such statements meaningful. Science could in principle have discovered a synchronicity between humanity and world, since there is nothing to rule out *a priori* the compatibility between mathematical physics and such a hypothesis (i.e. the hypothesis of a human species as old as the cosmos) – yet this would not have prevented us from raising the problem of dia-chronicity *in spite of it*. For the fundamental point is this: even if science had discovered this synchronicity, this would still have been a *discovery* – which is to say that it is precisely insofar as modern science is mathematized that it is capable of *raising* the question of a possible temporal hiatus between thinking and being – of construing the latter as a meaningful hypothesis, of giving it meaning, of rendering it tractable – whether in order to refute it or confirm it. It is precisely this capacity of scientific discourse which concerns us – its ability to give meaning to the possibility of the dia-chronic – not whether this possibility is confirmed or rejected. Ancestrality has allowed us to highlight the difficulty which modern philosophy has when it comes to thinking a certain type of contemporary scientific discourse – but what we are ultimately concerned with pertains to what seems to us to be the fundamental property or trait of *Galileism*, which is to say, of the mathematization of nature.

In order to properly grasp the nature of this property, it is necessary to understand in what regard Galileism endowed dia-chronic discourse with a hitherto unprecedented scope. Certainly, humans did not have to wait for the advent of empirical science in order to produce accounts of what had preceded human existence – whether in the shape of Cyclopes, Titans, or Gods. But the fundamental dimension presented by modern science from the moment of its inception was the fact that its assertions could become part of a *cognitive process*. They were no longer of the order of myths, theogonies, or fabulations, and instead became *hypotheses* susceptible to corroboration or refutation by actual experiments. The term 'hypothesis' here is not intended to suggest a kind of unverifiability that would be peculiar to such statements. We do not mean to imply the idea that no 'direct' verification of dia-chronic statements is possible by definition, since the occurrences to which they refer are posited as anterior or ulterior to the existence of human experience. For as a matter of fact, this absence of 'direct verification' holds for a great many scientific statements, if not for all of them, given that very few truths can be attained through immediate experience and that generally speaking, science is not based upon simple observations, but rather upon data that have already been processed and quantified by ever more elaborate measuring instruments. Thus, in qualifying the statements of empirical science as 'hypotheses', we do not seek to undermine their cognitive value but rather to confer upon them their full value as instances of knowledge. It is the discourse of empirical science which, for the first time, gives meaning to the idea of a rational *debate* about what did or did not exist prior to the emergence of humankind, as well as about what might eventually succeed humanity. Theories can always be improved and amended, but the very fact that *there can be* such dia-chronic theories is the remarkable feature made possible by modern knowledge. It was science that made it meaningful to disagree about what there might have been when we did not exist, and what there might be when we no longer exist – just as it is science that provides us with the means to rationally favour one hypothesis over another concerning the nature of a world without us.

But if science thereby renders dia-chronic knowledge possible, this is because it allows us to consider *all* of its statements – or at least all its statements about the inorganic – from a dia-chronic point of view. For the truth or falsity of a physical law is not established with regard to our own existence – whether we exist or do not exist has no bearing upon its truth. Certainly, the presence of an observer may eventually affect the effectuation of a physical law, as is the case for some of the laws of quantum physics – but the very fact that an observer can influence the law is itself a property of the law which is not supposed to depend upon the existence of an observer. Once again, the fundamental point at issue is not the fact that science is spontaneously realist, since the same could be said of every discourse, but rather the fact that science deploys a process whereby we are able to *know* what may be while we are not, and that this process is linked to what sets science apart: the mathematization of nature.

Let us try to be more precise about this. What fundamental change did Galileo bring about in our understanding of the link that ties mathematics to the world? There was nothing new about the geometrical description of phenomena, since Greek astronomy had already described stellar trajectories in geometrical terms. But these descriptions pertained to the 'immediately geometric' aspect of the phenomenon – what was subjected to mathematics was the unalterable form of a trajectory or a determinate surface area – in other words, a motionless expanse. Galileo, by way of contrast, conceives of movement itself in mathematical terms, and particularly the movement which appears to be the most changeable of all: the falling of terrestrial bodies. In doing so, he uncovered, beyond the variations of position and speed, the mathematical invariant of movement – that is to say, acceleration. From that point on, the world becomes *exhaustively* mathematizable – the mathematizable no longer designates an aspect of the world that is essentially immerged within the non-mathematizable (i.e. a surface or trajectory, which is merely the surface or trajectory of a moving body), it now indicates a world capable of autonomy – a world wherein bodies as well as their movements can be described independently of their sensible qualities, such as flavour, smell, heat, etc. The world of Cartesian extension is a world that acquires the independence of substance, a world that we can henceforth conceive of as indifferent to everything in it that corresponds to the concrete, organic connection that we forge with it – it is this *glacial* world that is revealed to the moderns, a world in which there is no longer any up or down, centre or periphery, nor anything else that might make of it a world designed for humans. For the first time, the world manifests itself as capable of subsisting without any of those aspects that constitute its concreteness for us.

It is this capacity whereby mathematized science is able to deploy a world that is *separable* from man – a capacity that Descartes theorized in all its power – that rendered possible the essential alliance between the Galilean and *Copernican* revolutions. In speaking of 'the Copernican revolution', what we have in mind is not so much the astronomical discovery of the decentring of the terrestrial observer within the solar system, but rather the much more fundamental decentring which presided over the mathematization of nature, viz., *the decentring of thought relative to the world within the process of knowledge*. The Galilean-Copernican revolution effectively consisted in the fact that *both* these events – astronomical decentring and mathematization of nature – were seized upon by their contemporaries as intimately corrected. And this correction in turn consisted in the fact that the mathematized world harboured within it what Pascal, on behalf of the libertine, had diagnosed as the eternal and frightening silence of infinite spaces – that is to say, the discovery that the world possesses a power of persistence and permanence that is completely unaffected by our existence or inexistence. From its inception, the mathematization of the world bore within it the possibility of uncovering knowledge of a world more indifferent than ever to human existence, and hence indifferent to whatever knowledge humanity might have of it. In this way, science carried within it the possibility of transforming every datum of our experience into a dia-chronic object – into a component of a world that gives itself to us as indifferent, in being what it is, to whether it is given or not. Thus, the Galilean-Copernican revolution has no other meaning than that of the paradoxical unveiling of thought's capacity to think what there is whether thought exists or not. The sense of desolation and abandonment which modern science instils in humanity's conception of itself and of the cosmos has no more fundamental cause than this: it consists in the thought of thought's contingency for the world, and the recognition that thought has become able to think a world that can dispense with thought, a world that is essentially unaffected by whether or not anyone thinks it.[1]

Let's clarify the sense of this latter assertion. We claimed that the dia-chronic statement expressed the very essence of modern science, insofar as the latter made it possible to integrate such statements into the realm of knowledge, as opposed to that of myth or fabulation. Such statements certainly do not claim that there could be no relation to the world other than the human relation to the world – we cannot prove that dia-chronic events could not have been the correlates of a non-human relation to their occurrence (i.e. we cannot prove that they were not witnessed by a god or by a living creature). But science's dia-chronic statements assume that the 'question of the witness' has become irrelevant to knowledge of the event. In other words, the decay of the radioactive material, or the nature of the stellar emission, are described in such a way that they must be assumed to be adequate to what we manage to think about them, while the question as to whether or not they were witnessed becomes irrelevant to the adequacy of this description. Or again: both this decay and this emission are conceived in such a way that they would have been identical to what we think about them even if human thought had never existed to think them. This is in any case a feasible hypothesis, which science renders meaningful, and which expresses the latter's general capacity to be able to formulate laws irrespective of the question of the *existence* of a knowing subject.

Thus, the decentring inherent in the Copernican-Galilean revolution proceeds by way of a Cartesian thesis, viz., *that whatever is mathematically conceivable is absolutely possible*. But it is important to note that the absolute here is not understood in terms of the capacity of mathematics to designate a referent that is assumed to be necessary or intrinsically ideal – rather, the absoluteness at issue here expresses the following idea: it is meaningful to think (even if only in a hypothetical register) that all those aspects of the *given* that are mathematically describable can continue to exist regardless of whether or not we are there to convert the latter into something that is given-to or manifested-for. Consequently, this dia-chronic referent may be considered *to be contingent while simultaneously being considered to be absolute*: it can be construed as an event, an object, or a processual stability, that need not be shown to be unconditionally necessary, since this would be contrary to our ontology. On the other hand, however, the meaning of the dia-chronic statement about a radioactive decay older than all terrestrial life is only conceivable if it is construed as absolutely indifferent to the thought that envisages it. Accordingly, the absoluteness of that which is mathematizable means: the possibility of factial existence outside thought – and not: the necessity of existence outside thought. Whatever is mathematizable can be posited hypothetically as an ontologically perishable fact existing independently of us. In other words, modern science uncovers *the speculative but hypothetical import* of every mathematical reformulation of our world. Consequently, the Galilean-Copernican decentring wrought by science can be stated as follows: what is mathematizable cannot be reduced to a correlate of thought.

Yet this is where we encounter a rather disconcerting paradox. This paradox is the following: when philosophers refer to the revolution in thought instituted by Kant as 'the Copernican revolution', they refer to a revolution *whose meaning is the exact opposite of the one we have just identified*. For as everyone knows, in the Preface to the second edition of the *Critique of Pure Reason*, Kant presents his own revolution in thought under the banner of the revolution wrought by Copernicus[2] – instead of knowledge conforming to the object, the Critical revolution makes the object conform to our knowledge. Yet it has become abundantly clear that a more fitting comparison for the Kantian revolution in thought would be to a 'Ptolemaic counter-revolution', given that what the former asserts is not that the observer whom we thought was motionless is in fact orbiting around the observed sun, but on the contrary, that the subject is central to the process of knowledge.[3] But what was the goal of this Ptolemaic revolution in philosophy, and what did it hope to achieve? What was the fundamental question on the basis of which the *1st Critique* reconfigured the whole of philosophy? It was the question about the conditions under which modern science is thinkable – *that is to say, the conditions of the Copernican revolution in the literal and genuine sense of the term*. In other words, the philosopher who placed the task of understanding the conditions of possibility for modern science at the heart of his project is also the philosopher who responded to this exigency by abolishing its initial condition – thus, *the Copernico-Galilean decentring carried out by modern science gave rise to a Ptolemaic counter-revolution in philosophy*. Even as thought realized for the first time that it possessed in modern science the capacity to actually uncover knowledge of a world that is indifferent to any relation to the world, transcendental philosophy insisted that the condition for the conceivability of physical science consisted in revoking all non-correlational knowledge of this same world.

It is important to underline the 'violence' of this contradiction, the extraordinary nexus that it seems to constitute: ever since the Kantian revolution, it has been incumbent upon 'serious' philosophers to think that *the condition for the conceivability of the Copernican decentring wrought by modern science is actually provided by a Ptolemaic re-centring of thought*. While modern science discovered for the first time thought's capacity to accede to *knowledge* of a world indifferent to thought's relation to the world, philosophy reacted to this discovery by discovering the naïvety of its own previous 'dogmatism', seeing in the 'realism' of pre-Critical metaphysics the paradigm of a decidedly outmoded conceptual naïvety. The philosophical era of correlation corresponds to the scientific era of decentring, and corresponds to it *as its very solution*. For it was in response to the very fact of science that philosophy embraced the various modes of correlation – science's decentring of thought relative to the world led philosophy to conceive of this decentring in terms of thought's unprecedented centrality relative to this same world. Since 1781 (the date of the 1st edition of the *Critique of Pure Reason*), to think science philosophically has been to maintain that *philosophical Ptolemaism harbours the deeper meaning of scientific Copernicanism.* Ultimately, philosophy maintains that the patently realist meaning of the claims of modern science is merely apparent, secondary, and derivative; the symptom of an attitude that is 'naïve' or 'natural' – admittedly, the latter is not merely the result of a simple 'error', since it belongs to the essence of science to adopt such an attitude – but once again, it is a derivative attitude, a mere offshoot of that primordial relation to the world which it falls to the philosopher to uncover.

Ever since Kant, to think science as a philosopher has been to claim that science harbours a meaning other than the one delivered by science itself – a meaning that is deeper, more originary, and that furnishes us with the truth of the latter. And this more originary meaning is correlational: it construes those elements that seem to be indifferent to our relation to the world in terms of that relation itself. It collapses the decentring wrought by science onto a centring which delivers its veritable meaning. The philosopher thereby claims to have also carried out what he calls, following Kant, his own 'Copernican revolution' – a claim which cannot but strike us as a fantastic obfuscation. In philosophical jargon, 'Copernican revolution' means that the deeper meaning of science's Copernican revolution is provided by philosophy's Ptolemaic counter-revolution. We will henceforth refer to this 'reversal of the reversal' as the 'schism' of modern philosophy, which expresses the following paradox: it is only since philosophy has attempted to think rigorously the revolution in the realm of knowledge brought about by the advent of modern science that philosophy has renounced the very thing that constituted the essence of this revolution; that is to say, science's non-correlational mode of knowing, in other words, *its eminently speculative character.*

It is worth lingering a little longer over the astonishing singularity of the Kantian revolution, whose repercussions continue to be felt among the philosophical community. This revolution consisted, first of all, in providing a decisive ratification of science's primacy over metaphysics in the realm of knowledge. It was Kant who succeeded in thinking – with a degree of radicality unmatched by any of his predecessors – science's promotion over metaphysics as privileged guarantor of knowledge. Henceforth, it is the man of science, rather than the metaphysician, who becomes, by Kant's own admission, the 'piston of knowledge'. Since Kant, metaphysics has been forced to revise its claim to be in possession of a theoretical knowledge of realities that are equal or even superior to those known by the sciences. And since Kant, philosophers in general have become willing to admit that science and science alone provides us with theoretical knowledge of nature, and that speculative meta-physics can no longer present itself as harbouring knowledge of a supposedly higher reality (i.e. cosmos, soul, or God) than the reality accessible to us by means of empirical science.

But science's promotion over philosophy as guarantor of knowledge has become the locus of a misunderstanding, not to say wrong-footing, that appears to be without precedent in the annals of thought – for it is at the very moment when philosophy attempted for the first time to think rigorously the primacy of scientific knowledge that it decided to abjure precisely that aspect of thought which constituted the revolutionary character of scientific knowledge: *its speculative import*. It is at the very moment when philosophy claimed to be acknowledging its own supersession by science in the realm of knowledge that it renounced as 'moth-eaten dogmatism' its own capacity to think the object 'in-itself' – precisely the mode of thinking that, for the first time, was concurrently being promoted to the status of potential knowledge in the context of this very science. Even as science, by virtue of its power of decentring, revealed to thought the latter's own speculative power, philosophy, at the very moment when it was ratifying this takeover, did so by abjuring all speculation, which is to say, by renouncing any possibility of thinking the nature of this revolution. Something akin to a 'catastrophe' occurred in this changeover from metaphysics to science as guarantor of knowledge – Copernican science provided the impetus for philosophy's abandonment of speculative metaphysics, but this abandonment was reflected back onto Copernican science as philosophy's Ptolemaic interpretation of the latter. Thus, philosophy's message to science was: 'it is you (and not speculative metaphysics) that holds the reins of knowledge, but the underlying nature of this knowledge is the very opposite of what it seems to you.' In other words, in providing the impetus for philosophy's destruction of speculative metaphysics, science also destroyed any possibility of a philosophical understanding of its own essence.

Moreover, far from being mitigated, this 'schism' has only been further 'aggravated' since Kant. For the more science has exhibited thought's actual capacity to probe ever more deeply into a world anterior to all humanity, the more 'serious' philosophy has exacerbated the correlational Ptolemaism inaugurated by Kant, continually tightening the ambit of the correlation while ascribing to this increasingly constrictive realm the true meaning of the ever expanding domain of scientific knowledge. While 'the man of science' has intensified the decentring due to scientific knowledge by uncovering diachronic occurrences of increasingly ancient provenance, 'the man of philosophy' has been narrowing the ambit of the correlation towards an originally finite 'being-in-the-world', or an epoch of Being, or a linguistic community; which is to say, an ever narrower 'zone', terrain, or habitat, but one of which the philosopher remains lord and master by virtue of the alleged singularity of her specific brand of knowledge. While the Copernican revolution has revealed its full extent, philosophers have accentuated their own pseudo-Copernican counter-revolution, remorselessly exposing the metaphysical naïvety of their predecessors by contracting the bounds of knowledge ever more stringently within the limits of humanity's present situation. And so it is that philosophers today vie with one another in terms of Ptolemaic narrowness while hoping to unveil the genuine meaning of a Copernican decentring whose scope has never seemed so vast or blindingly evident as it is now.

How did we arrive at this state of affairs? What happened in philosophy after Kant to render philosophers – *and only them, it seems* – incapable of understanding science's Copernican revolution as a *genuine* Copernican revolution? Why did philosophy not take the course exactly opposite to the one followed by transcendental or phenomenological idealism, viz., the course of a thought capable of accounting for the non-correlational scope of mathematics, which is to say, for the very existence of science, the latter being properly understood as the power to decentre thought? Why did philosophy, in attempting to think science, err towards transcendental idealism instead of resolutely orienting itself, as it should have, towards a *speculative materialism*? How is it that the most *urgent* question which science poses to philosophy has become, as far as philosophy itself is concerned, the *pointless* question *par excellence*, viz. *how is thought able to think what there can be when there is no thought*?

We should not be deceived: no correlationism, however insistent its anti-subjectivist rhetoric, is capable of thinking a dia-chronic statement without *destroying* its veritable meaning, and this at the very moment when it claims to have excavated its supposedly deeper meaning. The veritable meaning of the dia-chronic statement is indeed, as we have seen, its literal meaning, which must concurrently be thought as its deepest meaning. The meaning of the dia-chronic statement is: 'event X occurred at such and such time *prior to* the existence of thought' – and not, let us emphasize it: 'event X occurred prior to the existence of thought *for thought'*. The first statement does not claim that event X occurred prior to thought *for thought* – what it says is that thought *can think* that event X *can actually have occurred* prior to all thought, and indifferently to it. But no variety of correlationism, no matter how vehemently it insists that it should not be confused with subjective idealism *à la* Berkeley, can admit that this statement's literal meaning is also its deepest meaning. And as a matter of fact, once one has conceded that it makes no sense to claim that what *is* can be thought independently of the forms through which it is given to a thinking being, then it is no longer possible to accord to science that what it says is indeed the last word about what it says. It becomes impossible to assign to philosophy the task of grasping the ultimate meaning of science in science's dia-chronic statement, or of understanding how such a statement is possible *as* its ultimate meaning.

Thus, correlationism will have no option but to try to recapture this dia-chronicity of scientific discourse in terms of the alternative we examined earlier:

1. Either, this anteriority is only actually anterior to humanity insofar as it is the correlate of a thought that cannot be reduced to our empirical existence; in which case we proceed to eternalize the correlation in a manner comparable to Husserl's eternalization of the transcendental ego, which supposedly survives the death of every empirical ego.[4]
2. Or, the genuine meaning of this anteriority consists in its being no more than present thought's retrojection of a past that gives itself to thought as anterior to thought.

Since the first option (the eternalization of the correlation) would be tantamount to a return to metaphysics (the absolutization of the supposedly primordial determinations of subjectivity), correlationism in the strict sense will always opt for the second option, and hence for the retrojection of the dia-chronic past on the basis of the living present in which it is given. In this way, the schism of modernity – according to which the Ptolemaism of thought harbours the deeper meaning of the Copernicanism of science – reaches its apogee in this 'topsy-turvy' past, which has been trotted out and re-utilized in many different forms by thought. This is the ultimate expression of the schism: the deep meaning of the pre-human past consists in its being retrojected on the basis of a human present that is itself historically situated. While science, through its rigorous mathematization of nature, uncovered a time wherein humanity could come into existence or be abolished while that time remained unaffected, philosophical time has sought to demote the time of science to the level of a 'vulgar', 'derivative', or 'standardized' form of originary correlational temporality, being-in-the-world, or the relation to a supposedly primordial historicality.[5] And this transmutation of the dia-chronic past into a retrojective correlation exerts such a sway over thought today that it sometimes seems as though it encapsulated the modicum of knowledge philosophers can still lay claim to. You thought that what came before came before? Not at all: for there is a deeper level of temporality, within which what came before the relation-to-the-world is itself but a modality of that relation-to-the-world. It is this countersensical temporality that provides the originary sense for the naïve natural attitude espoused by non-philosophers, including those who are most knowledgeable. And the most marvellous thing of all about this whole business is that this becoming – in which what came before no longer comes before, and what comes after no longer comes after – allows whomever grasps its truth to propagate its counter-sense in such a way as to undermine every received idea. You think that a precursor is someone who comes before those who follow after? Well, you're wrong: the precursor is not the one who comes before, but rather the one whom the successors subsequently claim came before. Thus, the precursor *qua* precursor comes after her successors... This is the peculiar knowledge to which philosophers lay claim, a knowledge that sometimes seems to amount to little more than these rigmaroles wherein time is turned upside down, the better to contrive a countersensical redoubling of the time of science. A peculiar knowledge indeed, which renders us incapable of grasping precisely that which is actually most gripping about the temporality of science – the fact that science does indeed think that *what comes before comes before, and that what came before us came before us*. For it is precisely this power of thought and none other that constitutes the formidable *paradox of manifestation* uncovered by science, which philosophy should have been endeavouring to think during these past two centuries: how is empirical knowledge of a world anterior to all experience possible?[6]

Let us return to our original question: what is it that has kept this alternative course of thought blocked ever since Kant? Why did transcendentalism's rejection of speculative thought exert such an undivided sway over the realm of philosophy at the very moment when science called – as it had never done before – for the constitution of a form of speculation capable of identifying its conditions of possibility? What is the meaning of this 'Kantian catastrophe', of which contemporary correlationism is merely an exacerbated consequence?[7] Why have philosophers accommodated themselves for so long to this correlationist deception, which was supposed to provide them with the key to a scientific revolution that has continually contradicted their claims? We only have to listen to Kant for the answer: who was it that, by his own admission, 'woke' him from his 'dogmatic slumbers'?[8] Who encouraged him – and every subsequent correlationist – to relinquish every form of absolute in thought? Kant tells us explicitly: it was *David Hume* – that is to say, the problem of the causal connection as raised by Hume – or to put it more generally, *the destruction of the absolute validity of the principle of sufficient reason.*[9] It now becomes possible to identify the three fundamental stages of the Kantian 'catastrophe', as well as the nature of the deception which lies at its source:

1. The Copernico-Galilean event institutes the idea of a mathematical knowledge of nature – a nature that is henceforth stripped of its sensible qualities. It is Descartes who provides the initial philosophical ratification for the Galilean event. An initial equilibrium between physics and metaphysics is established through Descartes' rigorous distinction between the mathematical knowledge of nature and the knowledge of those *qualia* that are considered to be attributes of thinking alone. In short, it is Descartes who ratifies the idea that nature is devoid of thought (which is also to say that it is devoid of life, since the two are equivalent for him), and that thought is able to think this de-subjectivated nature *through* mathematics. But the absolute scope of mathematics is founded upon the metaphysical demonstration of a sovereign, perfect and supposedly veracious God who alone is able to guarantee the new science's capacity to know the truth.

2. However, as the Galileo-event unfolds, revealing the fallaciousness of all previous varieties of metaphysical knowledge, it also exposes the vanity of every attempt to provide a metaphysical foundation for physics. For the Galilean event does not only consist in the mathematical de-subjectivation of the world, but also in the destruction of every form of *a priori* knowledge of why the world is as it is. The idea that we could acquire definitive and necessary knowledge about what exists in this world – rather than having to be satisfied with reconstructing it as a fact – is gradually eroded as science exhibits its ability to destroy all previous

forms of knowledge – including those that had been proposed under the aegis of the new science, as was the case with Cartesian vortices. Thus, the Hume-event constitutes the second philosophical ratification of the Galileo-event by demonstrating the fallaciousness of all metaphysical forms of rationality, which is to say, by demonstrating the fallaciousness of the absoluteness of the principle of sufficient reason – thought must renounce every form of demonstration intended to establish *a priori* that whatever gives itself as being thus and so must unconditionally be thus and so. The world's being-thus-and-so can only be discovered by way of experience, it cannot be demonstrated to be absolutely necessary.

3. The Kant-event then exposes this collapse of metaphysics in its definitive and enduringly stable form by turning correlational knowledge into the only philosophically legitimate form of knowledge. Correlationism becomes the only licit form of philosophy as the henceforth *conditional* knowledge of our relation-to-the-world, which alone is capable of thinking science insofar as the latter has deposed speculative metaphysics, even though science itself has not renounced every form of universality. Since we can no longer accede to an unconditionally necessary truth of the kind sought for by Leibniz (whether in the form of an infinitely perfect God or the best of all possible worlds), we must renounce every variety of theoretical absolute, and content ourselves with uncovering the general conditions for the givenness of phenomena. In other words, in order to salvage the possibility of producing *a priori* statements, philosophy must dissociate the *a priori* from absolute truths, and construe it instead as the determination of the universal conditions of representation.

Accordingly, the deception that presides over this catastrophe is revealed to be what we earlier referred to as the 'de-absolutizing implication', that is to say, the idea that *there is an irrefutable inference from the end of metaphysics to the end of absolutes*. Since science has convinced us that all metaphysics is illusory, and since every absolute is metaphysical, then it follows that, in order to think science, we must renounce every form of absolute. But by the same token, we must also renounce the belief in the absolute scope of mathematics – the absolute scope that actually constitutes the very essence of the revolution in thought engendered by modern science. Thus, the Kantian catastrophe within whose parameters we continue to operate does indeed consist in renouncing every kind of absolute along with every variety of metaphysics.

Yet this was not what modern science actually required. Certainly, the latter's capacity to undermine all previous forms of knowledge enjoined us to stop believing that knowledge could demonstrate that a determinate reality must, absolutely and necessarily, be the way it is rather than some other way; but it also enjoined us to think that other mode of absoluteness that it had introduced for the first time into thought, in the form of the latter's Copernican decentring. And this is why, if we are to think the Galilean-Copernican fact of science without denaturing it further, we must think, as Descartes did, the speculative import of mathematics, but this time without relying, as he did, upon the metaphysical pretension to be able to prove the existence of a perfect being, which alone is supposedly capable of guaranteeing mathematics' own intrinsic mode of truth. Philosophy's task consists in re-absolutizing the scope of mathematics – thereby remaining, contrary to correlationism, faithful to thought's Copernican de-centring – but without lapsing back into any sort of metaphysical necessity, which has indeed become obsolete. It is a matter of holding fast to the Cartesian thesis – according to which whatever can be mathematized can be rendered absolute – without reactivating the principle of reason. And this seems to us to be the task of the principle of factiality, a task that is not only possible but also urgent: to derive, as a Figure of factiality, the capacity, proper to every mathematical statement, through which the latter is capable of formulating a possibility that can be absolutized, even if only hypothetically. It is a question of absolutizing 'the' mathematical just as we absolutized 'the' logical *by grasping in the fundamental criterion for every mathematical statement a necessary condition for the contingency of every entity.*

Clearly, then, our speculative reformulation of what we must now call 'Kant's problem' can be stated as follows: how is a mathematized science of nature possible? This problem can be broken down into two others, each of which concerns the speculative import of mathematics, but in a different way.

1. First, the speculative resolution of Kant's problem presupposes the factial resolution of the problem of ancestrality (or of dia-chronicity), which is to say, a demonstration to the effect that every mathematical statement – precisely insofar as it is mathematical – is not necessarily true, but absolutely possible. Thus, we must establish the following thesis, which we have already stated, by deriving it from the principle of factiality: what is mathematically conceivable is absolutely possible.

2. Moreover – and here we come back to our earlier discussion of the problem of the causal connection – the resolution of Kant's

problem presupposes that we have achieved *a speculative rather than merely hypothetical* resolution of Hume's problem. For it is also necessary to establish the legitimacy of the assumption that the stability of natural laws, which is the condition for every science of nature, can be *absolutized*. If empirical science is actually possible, we said, this is on account of the actual stability of the laws of nature. But it is now clear that this stability must be established as a mind-independent fact if we want to achieve a decisive break with contemporary Ptolemaism. Thus, it is a question of establishing that the laws of nature derive their factual stability from a property of temporality that is itself absolute, which is to say, from a property of time that is indifferent to our existence, viz., that of the non-totalizability of its possibilities. This is just to reiterate once more the need to establish the speculative scope of mathematics, but with one significant difference – it would no longer be a matter, here, of deriving the absolute *though* hypothetical scope of any mathematical statement whatsoever, but rather of deriving the absolute *and now unconditionally necessary* scope of a *particular* theorem, viz., the theorem that allows us to maintain the non-totalizability of the transfinite.

Consequently, we are faced with the requirement of a twofold absolutization of mathematics. The absolutization inherent in the problem of dia-chronicity basically asserts that every mathematical statement describes an entity which is essentially contingent, yet capable of existing in a world devoid of humanity – regardless of whether this entity is a world, a law, or an object. Accordingly, this is an absolutization that could be called *ontical*: it pertains to entities that are possible or contingent, but whose existence can be thought as indifferent to thought. By way of contrast, the absolutization of the Cantorian non-All requires an absolutization that is *ontological*, rather than ontical, because it now states something about *the structure of the possible as such*, rather than about this or that possible reality. It is a matter of asserting that the possible *as such*, rather than this or that possible entity, must *necessarily* be un-totalizable. Consequently, we are obliged to produce a factial derivation capable of establishing that, even if there are conceivable mathematical axiomatics that rule out the transfinite or disqualify the impossibility of a set of all sets, this does not imply that the non-All is merely one possibility among others. It must not imply that there are certain worlds whose possibilities are totalizable, while there are others whose possibilities are not. What must be demonstrated at this juncture is that only those theories that ratify the non-All harbour an ontological scope, while those others, which allow for some sort of conceivability of the All, would be merely ontical in scope, since the totality which they invoke, or the non-totality which they refuse to ratify, betray the fact that they are describing a totalizable entity, or a totalizable world, as opposed to the un-totalizable being of worlds.

It is clear then that the speculative resolution of Kant's problem will have to proceed by way of a derivation of the absolutizing scope of mathematics capable of resolving *both* the problem of dia-chronicity *and* that of Hume. The condition for the resolution of the first problem is a speculative resolution of the general problem – without which science loses its intrinsically Copernican sense; while the resolution of the second problem requires a non-metaphysical resolution of the general problem – without which science loses itself in the mysteries of real necessity. But both require a factial resolution of the problem, insofar as the factial is defined as the *very arena* for a speculation that excludes all metaphysics.

No doubt the question remains obscure in this formulation. But our goal here was not to tackle this resolution as such. Our only aim has been to try to convince the reader not only that it is possible to rediscover thought's absolutizing scope, but that it is urgent that we do so, given the extent to which the divorce between science's Copernicanism and philosophy's Ptolemaism has become abyssal, regardless of all those denials that serve only to perpetuate this schism. If Hume's problem woke Kant from his dogmatic slumber, we can only hope that the problem of ancestrality succeeds in waking us from our correlationist slumber, by enjoining us to reconcile thought and absolute.

Notes

Preface

1. 'The Philosophical Order' (*L'ordre philosophique*) is the name of the series co-edited by Badiou in which this book was first published in France by Editions du Seuil (translator).

Chapter 1: Ancestrality

1. Among the principal texts discussing this distinction we should mention René Descartes (1985a), *Meditations on First Philosophy* in J. Cottingham, R. Stoothoff, D. Murdoch (eds), *The Philosophical Writings of Descartes. Vol. II* (Cambridge: Cambridge University Press), Sixth Meditation; and Descartes (1985b), *The Principles of Philosophy* Article 1 and Article 4 [*Oeuvres complètes*, vol. IX, p. 57–62 (Paris: ed. Adam et Tannery, Vrin, 1996)], in *The Philosophical Writings of Descartes. Vol. I*, J. Cottingham, R. Stoothoff, D. Murdoch (eds) (Cambridge: Cambridge University Press), Second Part; John Locke (1979), *An Essay Concerning Human Understanding* (Oxford: Clarendon Press), Book 2, ch. 8. It goes without saying that Descartes and Locke do not understand this distinction in the same way, but we will focus here on a sense that seems to be common to both.

2. For reasons that we cannot examine here, Locke will add 'solidity' to this list. We should add that, from a strictly Lockean point of view, secondary qualities, like primary qualities, are intrinsic to perceptible bodies, since they correspond to the latter's capacity to engender in the mind sensible qualities which those bodies do not possess in themselves. But we are here following a common usage according to which secondary qualities are identified with sensible qualities, and thus dependent upon the relation between perception and the thing perceived.

3. On this point, see Alain Renaut's analysis of Kant's letter to Marcus Hertz dated 21 February 1772 in Renault (1997), *Kant aujourd'hui* (Paris: Aubier), ch. 1, pp. 53–77. For Berkeley's critique of the distinction between primary and secondary qualities see Berkeley (1998), *A Treatise Concerning the Principles of Human Understanding*, J. Dancy (ed.) (Oxford: Oxford University Press), Part One, Sections 8–10.

4. Cf. Hegel (1977), *The Phenomenology of Spirit*, tr. A.V. Miller (Oxford: Oxford University Press), Introduction, §85, p.54 (translation modified – translator).

5. Huneman, P. and Kulich, E. (1997), *Introduction à la phénoménologie* (Paris: Armand Colin), p. 22.

6. Francis Wolff (1997), *Dire le monde* (Paris: PUF), p. 11.

7. Wolff (1997), pp. 11–12.

8. Martin Heidegger (1969), *Identity and Difference*, tr. J. Stambaugh (New York: Harper and Row).

9. Heidegger (1969), 38. Heidegger insists that the 'co-' ('*zusammen*') in the term 'co-propriation' should be understood on the basis of belonging, rather than belonging being understood on the basis of the 'co-'. But this is simply a matter of avoiding the metaphysical understanding of the unity of thought and being as *nexus* or *connexio*, and the submission of everything to the order of the system. Thus it is not a question of abandoning the 'co-', but of rethinking its originary nature beyond the schemas of representation. On this point, see Heidegger (1969), pp. 29–33.

10. Martin Heidegger (1998a), 'On the Question of Being', in Pathmarks, W. McNeill (ed.) (Cambridge: Cambridge University Press), p. 308.

11. Dominique Lecourt recapitulates the basic elements of this history of absolute dating in the polemical context of the revival of creationism in 1980s America. Cf. Lecourt (1992), *L'Amerique entre la Bible et Darwin* [*America Between Darwin and the Bible*] (Paris: PUF), ch. IV, p. 100 and *passim*. On this point see also the French edition of *Scientific American: Pour la science, Le temps des datations*, January–March 2004. For a more technical introduction, see Roth, E. and Pouty, B. (1985), *Méthodes de datation par les phénomènes nucléaires naturels. Applications* [*Dating Methods Using Natural Nuclear Phenomena: Applications*] (Paris: Masson), particularly ch. 1.A (E. Roth: 'Principes, généralités') ['Principles and Generalities'], and ch. IX (G. Lalou and G. Valados: 'Thermoluminescence').

12. Although it is essentially distinct from the objection from the un-witnessed, the argument from ancestrality is nevertheless closer to the objection which points out that the singular birth and death of consciousnesses implies a time which cannot itself be of the order of consciousness. But

correlationism could defend itself against the latter by pointing out that one's individual birth and death occurs within a time which is woven from intersubjectivity – the time of the community of consciousnesses, which means that to be born and to die is to be born and to die for other consciousnesses, and hence to be deployed in a becoming which is once more reducible to its givenness for a community of egos. It is our conviction that this rejoinder is a desperate sophism, which reduces emergence and perishing to whatever the other perceives of it. But it is in order to avoid this loophole that we have restricted our argument to the ancestral, which rules out any recourse to community, but more importantly has the advantage of demonstrating that it is science which grants us access to a time which cannot be captured by any correlation.

13. We shall see in Chapter 5 of this book that Husserl and Heidegger registered this difference – although the unperceived never presented them with any serious difficulty, since it is synonymous with lacunary manifestation, they obviously considered the thought of a world devoid of all life to be a redoubtable challenge.

Chapter 2: Metaphysics, Fideism, Speculation

1. For this argument, see once again Descartes (1985a), Sixth Meditation, as well as Descartes (1985b), Second Part, 1st article.
2. Concerning the thinkability of the thing-in-itself, see Kant (1929), *Critique of Pure Reason*, tr. N. K. Smith (London: Macmillan), Preface to the Second Edition, B xxvi-xxvii, p. 27.
3. Kant (1929), A594/B622, p. 502.
4. G. W. Leibniz (1990), 'Monadology,' in *Philosophical Writings*, G. H. R. Parkinson (ed.) (London: J. M. Dent & Sons), §32, p. 184.
5. Cf. Descartes (1991), J. Cottingham, R. Stoothoff, D. Murdoch, A. Kenny (eds), *The Philosophical Writings of Descartes, Vol. III* (Cambridge: Cambridge University Press), letter to P. Mesland, 2 May 1644.
6. Concerning the point that the gods themselves (and hence thinking beings in general), although described as imperishable by Epicurus, must be conceived as essentially perishable, in contrast to elementary natures, see Marcel Conche (1987), *Épicure. Lettres et maximes* [*Epicurus: Letters and Maxims*] (Paris: PUF), Introduction, p. 44 and *passim*.
7. Ludwig Wittgenstein (1974), *Tractatus Logico-Philosophicus*, tr. D. F. Pears and B. F. McGuinness (London: Routledge), p. 73.
8. Wittgenstein (1974), p. 73. On this point see Wittgenstein (1966), 'Lecture on Ethics' in *Lectures and Conversations on Aesthetics, Psychology and Religious Belief*, C. Barrett (ed.) (Oxford: Basil Blackwell), pp. 53–72. See also Wittgenstein

(1979,) *Notebooks 1916–1916* (2nd edition), G. E. M. Anscombe and G. H. von Wright (eds) (Oxford: Basil Blackwell), entry dated 20.10.16: 'Aesthetically, the miracle is that the world exists. That there is what there is.' (86e).

9. Heidegger (1998b), 'Postscript to "What is Metaphysics"', in *Pathmarks*, W. McNeill (ed.) (Cambridge: Cambridge University Press), p. 234.

10. Concerning this twofold de-absolutization of the principles of non-contradiction and sufficient reason, see Wittgenstein (1974), 3.031; Heidegger (1996), *The Principle of Reason*, tr. R. Lilly (Bloomington and Indianapolis: Indiana University Press); and Heidegger (1994), *Grundsätze des Denkens* [*The Principles of Thought*], in *Gesamtausgabe, Band 79* (Frankfurt: Vittorio Klostermann).

11. I speak of 'naïve' realism and of 'speculative' idealism in order to underline the fact that, from within correlationism, the realist construal of the absolute is inevitably considered inferior to its idealist construal, since the former marks a break with every form of correlationism, while the latter acknowledges it sufficiently to absolutize it.

12. For an example of such a displacement of the status of non-contradiction carried out from within the Critical perspective, cf. Francis Wolff's particularly detailed analysis in Wolff (1997), pp. 21–69.

13. For an account of the originary and, according to us, enduring links between modern scepticism and fideism, see the classic study by Richard Popkin (2003), *The History of Scepticism: From Savanarola to Bayle* (Oxford: Oxford University Press), as well as the valuable work by Frédéric Brahami (2001), *Le travail du scepticisme. Montaigne, Bayle, Hume* [*The Work of Scepticism: Montaigne, Bayle, Hume*] (Paris: PUF).

14. Heidegger (1986), *Zürich Seminar* in *Gesamtausgabe, Band 15* (Frankfurt: Vittorio Klostermann). Concerning the parallel between Wittgenstein and Heidegger on the silence which the question of God imposes upon contemporary thought, cf. Jean-Luc Marion (1995), *God Without Being*, tr. T. A. Carlson (Chicago: University of Chicago Press), especially ch. 3, 'The Crossing of Being', pp. 53–107, where the original German text of Heidegger's 'Zürich Seminar' is reproduced and discussed.

15. We can only allude here to the predominant role played by fideism in the constitution of modern thought. This issue will be treated in greater depth in a forthcoming work in which we hope to develop the theoretical positions that we are merely sketching here, as well as their ethical consequences: *L'inexistence divine. Essai sur le dieu virtuel* [*Divine Inexistence: An Essay on the Virtual God*].

Chapter 3: The Principle of Factiality

1. See Aristotle (1928), *Metaphysica* in *The Works of Aristotle. Vol. VIII*, W. D. Ross (ed.) (Oxford: Clarendon Press), Γ.3, 1005^b, pp. 5–30.

2. For this demonstration, cf. Aristotle (1928), Γ.4.

3. See for example Leibniz (1990), §31–32, p. 184.

4. Cf. Newton C. A. Da Costa (1997), *Logiques classiques et non-classiques* (Paris: Masson).

5. ['Anything follows from a contradiction' – translator]

6. Meillasoux has coined the French neologisms *'factual'* and *'factualité'* to designate what he calls the 'non-factical' in such a way as to mark its distinction clearly from the ordinary meaning of the French *'factuel'* ('factual' in English). In order to provide an English rendering of this contrast between *'factuel'* and *'factual'* in French, I have decided to retain the word 'factual' for the French *'factuel'* but I have coined the English neologisms 'factial' and 'factiality' to translate Meillassoux's own French neologisms *'factual'* and *'factualité'*. This coinage is intended to indicate clearly the difference between the ordinary meaning of the word 'factual' in English and Meillassoux's philosophical meaning here. Existing terms such as 'factical' or 'facticity', which have been used to translate Heidegger's *'Faktizatät'*, cannot be used to render Meillassoux's *'factual'* or *'factualité'*, since Meillassoux also uses the former in their accepted Heideggerian sense precisely in order to contrast his own conception of absolute contingency to the more familiar Heideggerian notion of 'facticity' (translator).

7. When a student pointed out to him that there was a South American plant that did not correspond to his concept of a plant, Hegel is alleged to have replied that this was too bad – *for the plant*. cf. J-M. Lardic (1989) 'La contingence chez Hegel', in *Comment le sens commun comprend la philosophie* (Arles: Actes Sud). [The latter is a French edition of G. W. F. Hegel (2000), 'How the Ordinary Human Understanding Takes Philosophy (As Displayed in the Works of Mr. Krug', in *Between Kant and Hegel: Texts in the Development of Post-Kantian Idealism*, G. D. Giovanni and H. S. Harris (eds) (Indianapolis: Hackett), pp. 292–310. On the contingency of nature, see also G. W. F. Hegel (1970), *The Philosophy of Nature*, J. M. Perry (ed.) (London: Allen and Unwin), §248, 'Remark', p. 209; and §250, 'Remark', pp. 215–16 – translator]

8. On Hegel's notion of contingency, cf. the commentary cited in J. M. Lardic's note to Hegel's text on p. 108 of Lardic (1989). See also J. C. Pinson (1989), *Hegel, le droit et le libéralisme* (Paris: PUF), esp. chapters I and II; and Bernard Mabille (1999) *Hegel. L'épreuve de la contingence* (Paris: Aubier).

Chapter 4: Hume's Problem

1. For Hume's own formulation of the problem, see David Hume (1984), *A Treatise of Human Nature*, C. Mossner (ed.) (Harmondsworth: Penguin), Book I, Part III, pp. 117–229; and David Hume (1957), *Enquiry Concerning Human Understanding*, C. W. Hendel (ed.) (New York: Liberal Arts Press), Sections 4 and 5, pp. 40–68.

2. Popper clearly states his belief in the 'principle of the uniformity of nature': 'It never happens that old experiments one day yield new results. What happens is only that new experiments decide against an old theory.' Karl Popper (2002), *The Logic of Scientific Discovery* (London and New York: Routledge), pp. 249–50. The reason we insist on distinguishing Hume's problem from Popper's problem is because Popper himself considerably muddied the waters by referring to the problem of the future validation of scientific theories as 'Hume's problem'. Thus, Popper believed himself to be dealing with the issue that preoccupied Hume when in fact he was only dealing with a problem that assumes that the Humean difficulty *has already* been resolved. For Popper's question, which is to say the question of the future validity of our physical theories, assumes that in the future, even if those theories are refuted by new experiments, physics will still be possible, since such refutations will be carried out for the benefit of new physical theories. Thus Popper continues to assume that the principle of the uniformity of nature, which provides the condition for the possibility of physical experiments, will still be valid in the future, and it is by relying *a priori* on this supposedly necessary validity that he is able to elaborate the principles of his own epistemology.

3. Hume (1957), p. 44.

4. Hume (1957), p. 45.

5. In the 1st edition of the *Critique*, the objective deduction of the categories constitutes the third section of Chapter II in the 'Analytic of Concepts' (cf. Kant (1929), *Critique of Pure Reason*, tr. N. K. Smith (London: Macmillan), pp. 129–50); while in the 2nd edition of 1787, it takes up sections 15 to 24 of the same chapter – and even more specifically, sections 20 and 21 (cf. Kant (1929), pp. 151–75 and pp. 160–61). For a linear commentary of the objective deduction of 1781, cf. Jacques Rivelaygue (1992), *Leçons de métaphysique allemande. Tome II: Kant, Heidegger, Habermas* (Paris: Grasset), pp. 118–24.

6. Jean-René Vernes (1982), *Critique de la raison aléatoire, ou Descartes contre Kant* (Paris: Aubier), with a preface by Paul Ricoeur.

7. Vernes (1982), p. 45.

8. For a clear introduction to probability theory that covers both discrete

and continuous distributions (or finite and infinite numbers of possible cases respectively), cf. J.L. Boursin (1989) *Comprendre les probabilités* (Paris: Armand Colin).

9. Alain Badiou (2006), *Being and Event*, tr. O. Feltham (London: Continuum).

10. The reader should consult to the following 'Meditations' from *Being and Event*: 1–5, 7, 12–14, and most importantly, Meditation 26, which concerns the pluralization of infinite multiplicities.

11. Here is a simple example that may give non-mathematicians a better idea of Cantor's theorem. In the set-theoretical axiomatic, a set B is considered to be part of the set A if all the elements of B also belong to A. Consider the set A = (1, 2, 3), that is to say, a set comprising three elements. Now consider the set B, which comprises all the parts of A, and which can also be designated as p(A) – what are the elements of B? First of all, the set B contains the three singleton sets (1), (2) and (3) [a 'singleton' is a set comprising only one element – translator]. These parts of A are not identical with the elements of A (i.e. 1, 2 and 3), but with the grouping of these elements into sets containing them and them alone. These are the minimal parts of A – the parts comprising only one of the elements of A. Then we have parts in the usual sense of the term – those that comprise two of the three elements of A: (1, 2), (1, 3), (2, 3). Lastly, we have the maximal part of A, which is identical with A itself: (1, 2, 3). According to the set-theoretical definition of 'part', A is always part of itself, since all the elements of A do indeed belong to A. Finally, we would have to add the empty-set (whose existence standard set-theory posits, and whose uniqueness it demonstrates) to this list of the parts of A. The empty-set is part of every set, in the sense that the void, which has no elements, contains no elements that do not also belong to any set whatsoever (on this point, see Badiou's *Being and Event*, Meditation 7, pp. 86–92). A simple count then suffices to show that p(A) contains more elements than A itself (i.e. eight, rather than three elements). The power of Cantor's theorem resides in the way in which it generalizes this excess of the number of groupings of a set over the number of its elements to any set whatsoever, even infinite ones – whence the impossibility of halting the proliferation of infinities, since for any set whose existence we assume, we also assume the existence of its quantitative surpassing by the set of its parts.

12. [Translation modified.]

13. This surpassing of the proper limits of aleatory reason is just as evident in the famous passage about cinnabar, where Kant, having just hypothetically assumed the absence of necessity in the laws of nature, infers what

the consequences of this contingency would be for nature: 'If cinnabar were sometimes red, sometimes black, sometimes light, sometimes heavy, if a man changed sometimes into this and sometimes into that animal form, if the country on the longest day were sometimes covered with fruit, sometimes with ice and snow, my empirical imagination would never find opportunity when representing red colour to bring to mind heavy cinnabar.' (Kant 1929: 132, A 100). That it is indeed a frequent modification ('the longest day' sufficing to produce numerous chaotic occurrences) which is posited here as the *consequence* of the contingency of laws, is shown by the goal of the argument from cinnabar. For Kant, in this passage, it is a matter of demonstrating the absurdity of trying to explain, as Hume does, the necessity of natural laws solely in terms of our subjective habituation to the latter. For unless such objective necessity pre-existed the habituation which it induces in us, we would never have had occasion, Kant maintains, to become habituated to any event whatsoever, given the absence of *sufficiently stable* regularities in the empirical data.

Chapter 5: Ptolemy's Revenge

1. Contrary to what is often claimed, the end of Ptolemaic astronomy does not mean that humanity felt itself humiliated because it could no longer think of itself as occupying the centre of the world. In actuality, the centrality of the earth was then considered to be a shameful rather than glorious position in the cosmos – a kind of sublunary rubbish dump. On this point cf. Rémi Brague (2004), *The Wisdom of the World: The Human Experience of the Universe in Western Thought*, tr. T. Lavender Fagan (Chicago: University of Chicago Press). The successive upheavals brought about by the mathematization of nature are better understood as resulting from the loss of every privileged point of view and from the dissolution of the ontological hierarchization of places. Humanity becomes unable to invest the world with the meaning that had hitherto allowed it to inhabit its environment – the world can do without humanity, and consequently the latter becomes 'superfluous', as Sartre puts it. We should also add that when we speak of 'Galileism' we have in mind the general movement of the mathematization of nature initiated by Galileo, rather than the ideas of the latter *per se*, since these continued to be suffused with Platonism and did not by themselves represent a complete break with the conception of the cosmos held by the Ancients. On both these points – the mathematization of nature in the modern era and the thought of Galileo – the work of Alexandre Koyré remains indispensable. See in particular Koyré

(1968), *From the Closed World to the Infinite Universe* (Baltimore: Johns Hopkins), and Koyré (1985), *Études d'histoire de la pensée scientifique* (Paris: Gallimard).

2. Cf. Kant (1929), p. 25, Bxxiii.

3. On this point, see for example Renaut (1997), pp. 68–9.

4. Concerning Husserl's eternalization of the ego, see Husserl (2002), 'Foundational Investigations of the Phenomenological Origin of the Spaciality of Nature: The Originary Ark: The Earth Does Not Move', in *Husserl at the Limits of Phenomenology*, L. Lawlor and B. Bergo (eds) (Evanston, IL: Northwestern University Press). This is a highly significant text because it clearly exhibits the Ptolemaic reduction of science's Copernicanism which is inherent in every correlationist approach. Of particular relevance here is the passage concerning the phenomenological interpretation of the hypothesis of the destruction of all life on earth following a stellar impact: 'What sense could the collapsing masses in space, in one space constructed *a priori* as absolutely homogenous, have, if the constituting life were eliminated? Indeed, does that elimination itself have the sense, if it has any at all, of an elimination of and in the constituting subjectivity? The ego lives and precedes all actual and possible beings [...]' Husserl (2002), p. 131.

5. Obviously, what we have in mind here is primarily – but not exclusively – Heidegger's conception of temporality. It should also be mentioned here that Heidegger's debt to phenomenology – a debt that he never entirely discharged – seems to have driven him towards a highly problematic 'correlationism of finitude' wherein the world and our relation-to-the-world, man and nature, being and its shepherd, are construed as fundamentally indissociable terms, destined to 'subsist' or (perhaps?) perish together. In this regard, it seems apposite to quote the following enigmatic but also telling observation by Heidegger: 'I often ask myself – this has for a long time been a fundamental question for me – what nature would be without man – must it not resonate through him [*hindurchschwingen*] in order to attain its ownmost potency?' Letter dated 11 October 1931 to Elizabeth Blochmann in *Martin Heidegger – Elisabeth Blochmann. Briefwechsel 1918–1969*, Joachim W. Storck (ed.) (Marbach am Neckar: Deutsches Literatur-Archiv), p. 44, 1990.

6. These analyses probably bear some resemblance to those developed at much greater length in the first section of the fourth part of Paul Ricoeur's *Time and Narrative: Vol. III*, tr. D. Pellauer and K. Blamey (Chicago: University of Chicago Press, 1990), which is entitled 'The Aporetics of Temporality'. Nevertheless, any reader consulting Ricoeur's text should

have little difficulty noticing the fundamental differences between our two perspectives (most notably with regard to the interpretation of Kant), the most important of which is also the most obvious – viz., that while Ricoeur's approach is aporetic, ours is speculative.

7. This is a 'catastrophe' whose ramifications would need to be studied within Kant's work itself, and principally through the tension that the *1st Critique* (1781) retrospectively imparts onto our understanding of Kant's *Universal Natural History and Theory of the Heavens*, tr. S. L. Jaki (Edinburgh: Scottish Academic Press, 1981), published in 1755 and conceived during his pre-Critical period. Kant's cosmogony of 1755 assumed that the cosmos had a history anterior to every witness – except for God and his angels. But having taken the Critical turn, how is Kant to conceive of the truth of such a history, given that God is no longer an object of theoretical knowledge? This difficulty cannot be obviated by claiming that this truth is to be construed merely as a regulative Idea, for the intelligible content of this Idea is that of a world un-witnessed by any human subject (given that the initial conditions of matter at the beginnings of the world obviously rule out the possibility of human existence). Consequently, either this Idea refers back to a mechanical spatio-temporal occurrence devoid of any subject for whom this space-time constitutes a possible form of intuition, which is to say that this occurrence simply becomes unintelligible from the perspective of the Critical philosophy; or it is a condition of its intelligibility that it indexes the presence of an eternal witness capable of converting it into a correlational occurrence. But since such a witness becomes inaccessible to theoretical cognition after 1781, only *practical* reason, which is the moral guarantor for the existence of God – in other words, only the *2nd Critique* – can preserve the intelligibility of this cosmogony. Descartes claimed that an atheist mathematician could never be absolutely certain of her demonstrations; similarly, would it not be necessary to claim that a Kantian astronomer who was insufficiently moral to believe in God would be incapable of founding the validity of her science ...? On the relations between Kant's *Critique* and his *Universal Natural History*, cf. Paul Clavier (1997), *Kant. Les idées cosmologiques* (Paris: PUF).

8. Kant (1950), *Prolegomena to Any Future Metaphysics*, L. W. Beck (ed.) (New York: Liberal Arts Press), p. 8.

9. Michel Puech (1990) questions the historical value of such an avowal – without undermining its philosophical relevance – in *Kant et la causalité. Étude sur la formation du sytème critique* (Paris: Vrin).

Bibliography

Aristotle (1928) *Metaphysica*, in *The Works of Aristotle. Vol. VIII*, W. D. Ross (ed.) (Oxford: Clarendon Press)

Badiou, A. (2006) *Being and Event*, tr. O. Feltham (London: Continuum)

Berkeley, G. (1998) *A Treatise Concerning the Principles of Human Understanding*, J. Dancy (ed.) (Oxford: Oxford University Press)

Blochmann, E. and Heidegger, M. (1990) *Martin Heidegger – Elisabeth Blochmann. Briefwechsel 1918–1969*, Joachim W. Storck (ed.) (Marbach am Neckar: Deutsches Literatur-Archiv)

Boursin, J. L. (1989) *Comprendre les probabilités* (Paris: Armand Colin)

Brague, R. (2004) *The Wisdom of the World: The Human Experience of The Universe in Western Thought*, tr. T. Lavender Fagan (Chicago: University of Chicago Press)

Brahami, F. (2001) *Le travail du scepticisme. Montaigne, Bayle, Hume* (Paris: PUF)

Clavier, P. (1997) *Kant. Les idées cosmologiques* (Paris: PUF)

Conche, M. (1987) *Épicure. Lettres et maximes* (Paris: PUF)

Da Costa, N. C. A. (1997) *Logiques classiques et non-classiques* (Paris: Masson)

Descartes, R. (1985a) *Meditations on First Philosophy*, in J. Cottingham, R. Stoothoff, D. Murdoch (eds), *The Philosophical Writings of Descartes. Vol. II* (Cambridge: Cambridge University Press)

—— (1985b) *The Principles of Philosophy*, in *The Philosophical Writings of Descartes. Vol. I*, J. Cottingham, R. Stoothoff, D. Murdoch (eds) (Cambridge: Cambridge University Press)

—— (1991) *The Philosophical Writings of Descartes. Vol. III*, J. Cottingham, R. Stoothoff, D. Murdoch, A. Kenny (eds) (Cambridge: Cambridge University Press)

Hegel, G. W. F. (1970) *The Philosophy of Nature*, J. M. Petry (ed.) (London: Allen and Unwin)

—— (1977) *The Phenomenology of Spirit*, tr. A.V. Miller (Oxford: Oxford University Press)

—— (2000) 'How the Ordinary Human Understanding Takes Philosophy (As Displayed in the Works of Mr. Krug', in *Between Kant and Hegel: Texts in the Development of Post-Kantian Idealism*, G. D. Giovanni and H. S. Harris (eds) (Indianapolis: Hackett)

Heidegger, M. (1969) *Identity and Difference*, tr. J. Stambaugh (New York: Harper and Row)

—— (1986) *Zürich Seminar*, in *Gesamtausgabe, Band 15* (Frankfurt: Vittorio Klostermann)

—— (1994) *Grundsätze des Denkens*, in *Gesamtausgabe, Band 79* (Frankfurt: Vittorio Klostermann)

—— (1996) *The Principle of Reason*, tr. R. Lilly (Bloomington and Indianapolis: Indiana University Press)

—— (1998a) 'On the Question of Being', in *Pathmarks*, W. McNeill (ed.) (Cambridge: Cambridge University Press).

—— (1998b) 'Postscript to "What is Metaphysics"', in *Pathmarks*, W. McNeill (ed.) (Cambridge: Cambridge University Press)

Hume, D. (1957) *Enquiry Concerning Human Understanding*, C. W. Hendel (ed.) (New York: Liberal Arts Press)

—— (1984) *A Treatise of Human Nature*, C. Mossner (ed.) (Harmondsworth: Penguin)

Huneman, P. and Kulich, E. (1997) *Introduction à la phénoménologie* (Paris: Armand Colin)

Husserl, E. (2002) 'Foundational Investigations of the Phenomenological Origin of the Spatiality of Nature: The Originary Ark, The Earth, Does Not Move', in *Husserl at the Limits of Phenomenology*, L. Lawlor and B. Bergo (eds) (Evanston, IL: Northwestern University Press)

Kant, I. (1929) *Critique of Pure Reason*, tr. N. K. Smith (London: Macmillan)

—— (1950) *Prolegomena to Any Future Metaphysics*, L.W. Beck (ed.) (New York: Liberal Arts Press)

—— (1981) *Universal Natural History and Theory of the Heavens*, tr. S. L. Jaki (Edinburgh: Scottish Academic Press)

Koyré, A. (1968) *From the Closed World to the Infinite Universe* (Baltimore: Johns Hopkins)

—— (1985) *Études d'histoire de la pensée scientifique* (Paris: Gallimard)

Lalou, G. and Valados, G. (1985) 'Thermoluminescence', in E. Roth and B. Pouty (eds) *Méthodes de datation par les phénomènes nucléaires naturels. Applications* (Paris: Masson)

Lardic, J. M. (1989) 'La contingence chez Hegel', in *Comment le sens commun comprend la philosophie* (Arles: Actes Sud)

Lecourt, D. (1992) *L'Amérique entre la Bible et Darwin* (Paris: PUF)

Leibniz, G. W. (1990) *Monadology*, in *Philosophical Writings*, G. H. R. Parkinson (ed.) (London: J. M. Dent & Sons)

Locke, J. (1979) *An Essay Concerning Human Understanding* (Oxford: Clarendon Press)

Mabille, B. (1999) *Hegel. L'épreuve de la contingence* (Paris: Aubier)

Marion, J.-L. (1995) *God Without Being*, tr. T. A. Carlson (Chicago: University of Chicago Press)

Meillassoux, Q. (forthcoming) *L'inexistence divine. Essai sur le dieu virtuel*

Popkin, R. (2003) *The History of Scepticism: From Savanarola to Bayle* (Oxford: Oxford University Press)

Popper, K. (2002) *The Logic of Scientific Discovery* (London and New York: Routledge)

Puech, M. (1990) *Kant et la causalité. Étude sur la formation du système critique* (Paris: Vrin)

Renaut, A. (1997) *Kant aujourd'hui* (Paris: Aubier)

Ricoeur, P. (1990) *Time and Narrative: Vol. III*, tr. D. Pellauer and K. Blamey (Chicago: University of Chicago Press)

Rivelaygue, J. (1992) *Leçons de métaphysique allemandes. Tome II: Kant, Heidegger, Habermas* (Paris: Grasset)

Roth, E. and Pouty, B. (eds) (1985) *Méthodes de datation par les phénomènes nucléaires naturels. Applications* (Paris: Masson)

Vernes, J. R. (1982) *Critique de la raison aléatoire, ou Descartes contre Kant* (Paris: Aubier)

Wittgenstein, L. (1966) 'Lecture on Ethics', in *Lectures and Conversations on Aesthetics, Psychology and Religious Belief*, C. Barrett (ed.) (Oxford: Basil Blackwell)

—— (1974) *Tractatus Logico-Philosophicus*, tr. D. F. Pears and B. F. McGuinness (London: Routledge)

—— (1979) *Notebooks 1916–1916,* (2nd edition), G. E. M. Anscombe and G. H. von Wright (eds.) (Oxford: Basil Blackwell)

Wolff, F. (1997) *Dire le monde* (Paris: PUF)

Index of Concepts

Index of Names